P9-AEZ-314

claudia's cocina

claudia's cocina
A TASTE OF MEXICO

claudia sandoval

EDITED BY LEDA SCHEINTAUB

PHOTOGRAPHY & STYLING BY
TODD PORTER AND DIANE CU-PORTER

Stewart, Tabori & Chang | New York

Published in 2016 by Stewart, Tabori & Chang
An imprint of ABRAMS

MasterChef is a trademark of Shine Television, LLC and used under license.
The MasterChef logo is a trademark of Shine Limited and used under license.
All rights reserved. MasterChef is based on a format created by Franc Roddam
in association with Ziji Productions.

Library of Congress Control Number: 2015949318

ISBN: 978-1-61769-189-8

Editor: Samantha Weiner
Designer: Danielle Young
Production Manager: True Sims

The text of this book was composed in Benton Sans, Brandon Grotesque,
and Thirsty Rough.

Printed and bound in the United States

10 9 8 7 6 5 4 3 2 1

FOX™ Fox and its related
entities. All rights reserved.

ABRAMS
THE ART OF BOOKS SINCE 1949
115 West 18th Street
New York, NY 10011
www.abramsbooks.com

PARA TI MADRE,
FOR YOU YANI,
Y PARA USTEDES
ABUELAS COTI Y HERMELINDA

contents

CONTENIDO

foreword

What exactly is a MasterChef? Is it someone who has mastered the art of cooking? Someone who can properly run a professional kitchen? Maybe it's someone who can think outside the (mystery) box and handle large amounts of pressure (tests). The truth is, it's a combination of all the above. This past season, after whittling down the best home cooks from literally thousands of people across the country, Gordon Ramsay, Christina Tosi, and I finally decided on the one person who was deserving of this title—her name was Claudia Sandoval.

In this, her first-ever book, Claudia takes us inside her *cocina*, showing us the ins and outs of her style of cooking, a style that is as authentic as it is delicious. From dishes rooted in classical Mexican cuisine to fun and creative takes on Southern California fare, Claudia shows that one of the most important things people can do in the kitchen is find their own voice. The great news is that she clearly has done just that. The recipes included in this book scream at the top of their lungs with flavor and hit nothing but high notes!

People often ask us judges, "How did you decide on the winner?" Obviously there is a ton of discussion, debating, splitting hairs, and going back and forth, highlighting the pros and cons of the finalists and their respective time spent in the *MasterChef* kitchen. But at the end of the day, we ask ourselves a couple of questions. Whose house or restaurant would we want to dine in tonight? Whose book would we want to go out and buy tomorrow? This season, time and time again it was Claudia's name that came up.

With that said, there was something else that we all noticed as well. While some contestants excelled in particular styles or cuisines, Claudia was so well-rounded that she could jump from an amazing layer cake in one challenge to an awe-inspiring dish she seemed to pull out of nowhere in a mystery box challenge. When it came to the finale, we realized the amazing fact that not only did Claudia possess the ability to make her *own* authentic dishes, but she could also cook the food the other contestants were serving. Meanwhile, no other contestant was able to replicate Claudia's food, and this set her far apart from the rest.

All of that skill, technique, and creativity is what helped Claudia be crowned America's next MasterChef, and that is the reason why you are now holding her book in your hands. It is more than simply a cookbook; it is a living document of Claudia's culinary journey. The recipes are chock-full of heart and soul, each displaying flavors and techniques that you'll keep with you in your foodie toolbox for years to come.

Let the pages guide you through the rich history of her cooking style. Use it as a reference for the classics or as a jumping-off point as you create something of your very own. Cookbooks are most useful when they are seen as an inspirational blueprint. Just as Claudia was able to find her own voice through cooking, you too can discover your own style through the experience of *Claudia's Cocina*.

—Graham Elliot

introduction

INTRODUCCIÓN

"AT THE END OF THE DAY, WE CAN ENDURE MUCH MORE THAN WE THINK WE CAN." —FRIDA KAHLO

It is often said that dreamers are the only people who actually get to fulfill their dreams. Today I still feel like I am dreaming.

I remember feeling negative and defeated in the days leading up to the *MasterChef* auditions. I was drumming up every single excuse I could to continue living my paycheck-to-paycheck life. I was a single mom who provided a living for her daughter and was still striving to find her place in the professional world and in life. With no savings, no childcare, and little hope in my heart, I tried to convince myself that I couldn't afford to take that kind of risk. When I think back to that time now, I see how close I was to letting fear dictate my life.

No mas! (No more!) It was time for a change. My creativity was stagnant and I was craving the opportunity to show the world what I was capable of. I just had to take that chance. The months spanning from the audition to the train ride to Los Angeles passed in a hurried and emotional blink of the eye. I walked away from my daughter at four in the morning as she cried and begged me not to leave. But I was determined.

A single mother raised me. A mother who never faltered in going to work, making a living, and keeping food in our bellies and a roof over our heads. A mother who taught me the value of never giving up, dusting yourself off, and keeping your chin up high toward the sky. She embodied hope and never allowed us to fret.

While my heart broke that morning, I knew that I had one mission. I needed to win. Not only because it would change our lives forever, but because taking this opportunity would show my daughter and others that we cannot continue to hold ourselves back. We cannot continue to allow fear and complacency to stymie us and keep us from our true passions and calling. We must rise above the negativity cloud and

into the open air of full-fledged flight. Had I not left that day, I would not be writing this book.

It is still so very profound to sit here and wrap my head around the fact that Chef Ramsay called my name at the end of the finale. I battled what I believe to be the best group of competitors the *MasterChef* kitchen has seen. Every day I persevered and smiled, even when I was feeling tired, depressed, and homesick. Frida Kahlo was right: we truly can "endure much more than we think we can."

This book is about so much more than recipes. It is a telling of my family's history, and it shares not just a taste of Mexico but also a taste of the journey that I have lived in life. From the prickly cactus to the sweet desserts, my life, like many of yours, has been riddled with ups and downs and trials and tribulations.

I hope that this book does a couple of things. I hope it reminds you that you should never be ashamed of where you come from, but rather celebrate every bit of who you are. I hope it encourages you to stop making excuses and push the boundaries of your fears and day-to-day life. And I hope that it inspires you to cook food that doesn't always look pretty but that warms your soul. Food that isn't a quick fix, but rather a labor of love shared with family and friends. Meals that bring you together, remind you why you work so hard every day, and why you deserve everything amazing in this world.

Provecho, familia.

Claudia Sandoval

the basics

LO BASICO

Learning the basics is where all good cooks start. You have to have a good foundation if you are going to have a great structure. So I wanted to take you through the most important basics you will need to make some of the most delicious Mexican meals. Many of these are recipes that people have long asked for from my mom. Luckily, I was able to convince her to share them with you in this book.

These basic recipes include everything from cleaning cactus to making flour tortillas, which as many of you may know can be quite difficult. Fortunately, my mom and I decided to show you step-by-step how we go about making these delightful accompaniments to any meal. Some of these "basics" take more than just a couple of tries to master, as evidenced by my years of practice, but stick with it and you will do just fine!

Cleaning cactus is no easy feat to accomplish. In fact, I was too scared to attempt it until I was older, for fear of getting pricked. That's because even though the bigger needles are visible to the naked eye, there are also some tiny needles that are as clear as water and virtually invisible.

You can blanch your cactus, boil it, sauté it, or even cure it in salt (see page 37) for a different approach. Heck, some people blend cactus into their green smoothies. Note that the smaller the paddle, the more tender the cactus will be.

In this book, I've shared two of my favorite cactus-centered recipes, Cactus Salsa (page 37) and Cactus and Queso Fresco Salad (page 132).

how to prepare cactus paddles

COMO PREPARAR NOPALES

here is what you will need:

Medium bowl

Tongs

Cactus paddles

Vegetable peeler

Cutting board

Chef's knife or paring knife

Baking dish filled with water

✣ To begin, invert the medium bowl so the dome is facing upward. Using tongs, place a cactus paddle over the bowl and, using a vegetable peeler, remove the cactus needles. It is OK to take off a bit of the green skin in the process, but you want to try to avoid losing too much of the cactus. Position any part of the paddle that is hard to reach over the domed area of the bowl, using the contour of the bowl to help the peeler remove the needles.

✣ Lay a cactus paddle flat on the cutting board and use your tongs to hold the paddle in place. Cut ½ to 1 inch (12 mm to 2.5 cm) off of the base of the cactus. Then rotate the cactus, trimming ¼ to ½ inch (6 to 12 mm) off of the edges all the way around. Once you're done, remove the edges from the cutting board and discard them.

✣ When your cactus paddles are clean and trimmed, place them in the baking dish filled with water (this will remove some of the slime released by the cactus) until you're ready to use them.

If you are going to learn one thing from me, it's how to make great beans. Nothing screams Mexican food like beans, right? So I am going to share my family's simple way of making *frijoles de la olla* (boiled beans), which go well with braised meat dishes of all types and are the foundation for our Traditional Refried Beans (page 143).

When I was growing up, every Sunday my mom would boil a large pot of beans for the week ahead. This is that same simple recipe that I learned more than twenty-five years ago, and as simple as it may be, it is very important to follow every step carefully, as doing so will give you the best flavor and the correct texture.

boiled beans

FRIJOLES DE LA OLLA

makes about 10½ cups (2.6 ℒ)

4 cups (780 g) dried pinto or Peruvian beans

5 quarts (4.7 L) hot water

1¼ tablespoons salt

⊁ Spread the beans on a counter or table and sort out any broken or damaged beans. Place the beans in a large colander and rinse under cold running water for 2 to 3 minutes, moving the beans around with your hands to make sure all sand particles are washed away.

⊁ Add the beans and hot water to a large stockpot. Place it over high heat, cover, and bring it to a boil (if the water bubbles over, uncover and stir the beans, then cover again and lower the heat if needed). Reduce the heat to medium and boil for an additional 20 minutes, checking the water level every 7 to 10 minutes and adding water to return the water level to where it originally was if needed. Boil until a bean can be squished between your pointer finger and thumb with ease and the beans are smooth in texture and not grainy on the tongue. Turn off the heat, add the salt, and stir with a large spoon. Cover and allow them to rest for 15 minutes before scooping out and serving or using to refry. Cooked beans will keep for about 1 week in the fridge or up to 4 months in the freezer (store them in their cooking liquid).

notes

This method of boiling beans at a high temperature is the fastest way of cooking beans and is what I use for beans that are going to be refried. For perfectly shaped beans, you've got to soak the beans overnight, drain the soaking water, add fresh water, and cook the beans at a simmer for about 1½ hours. Remember, the key is to keep the lid on the whole time (except when adding water) and to make sure not to salt the beans until they are off the heat.

You can add extra flavor to the beans by including a whole peeled onion or some peeled garlic cloves in the cooking liquid.

Corn tortillas were one of the first recipes I learned to make. It's one of those basic recipes that all Mexican children grow up learning. In fact, teaching my Munchkin made for some of the most memorable kitchen experiences we've had together.

Fresh corn tortillas are easy to make, but I must warn you: fresh masa has a very different consistency from packaged instant corn masa flour. It is denser and the texture is smooth and starchy. If possible, use fresh ground masa for the best corn flavor.

corn tortillas

TORTILLAS DE MAÍZ

makes thirty-two 6-inch (15-cm) tortillas

FOR FRESH MASA TORTILLAS:

¾ teaspoon salt

2 pounds (910 g) fresh unsalted ground corn masa

¼ teaspoon fresh lime juice

FOR DRIED MASA TORTILLAS:

¾ teaspoon salt

4 cups (520 g) instant corn masa flour, such as Maseca

¼ teaspoon fresh lime juice

⇘ If you're using fresh masa for your tortillas, combine all the ingredients in a bowl and knead until incorporated.

⇘ If you're making dried masa tortillas, first whisk the salt into the corn flour, then add 3 cups (720 ml) warm water and the lime juice and mix until incorporated. If the masa is too sticky or wet, add a bit more masa flour and continue kneading until it is easy to manage. Allow the masa to rest in the refrigerator for 20 to 30 minutes before proceeding.

⇘ For either masa dough: Divide the masa into four equal portions and place them in a bowl; cover with a damp towel to keep your masa from developing a dry crust.

⇘ Preheat a griddle or *comal* (tortilla griddle) over medium-high heat.

⇘ Cut through both sides of a large plastic bag, preferably a produce bag from the grocery store (see Notes), from the opening of the bag to the bottom edge (do not cut past the seam) to create a long strip of plastic with the seam down the middle. Lay the plastic flat on your tortilla press with the seam at the joint of the tortilla press. There will be extra plastic bag by the handle, but don't worry; you will be using it to retrieve the tortilla later.

⊱ Divide the first portion of masa into eight equal-size balls. Place a ball onto the middle of the lined tortilla press. Cover the tortilla ball with the plastic, leaving the seam near the joint of the press, and press down to close the tortilla press. Be careful not to press too hard, as you don't want to make your tortilla too thin (see Notes). Don't be afraid to take a peek.

⊱ Open the tortilla press. Remove the plastic from the press, lay the tortilla facedown on one hand, and carefully peel back the top layer of plastic. Place your other hand on the tortilla and flip the tortilla onto that hand. Carefully peel back the plastic again, removing it completely and leaving the tortilla on your hand.

⊱ In one sweeping motion, almost as if you were going to brush the back of your hand over the griddle, carefully lay the tortilla on the griddle, taking care not to burn yourself. This sweeping motion will ensure there are no marks on the tortilla from flipping it once again.

⊱ Cook the tortilla for 1 minute on each side, or until it puffs up, flipping the tortilla with your hands or a spatula if you aren't familiar with the heat of a griddle. Remove the tortilla from the griddle and wrap it in a kitchen towel or place it in a tortilla warmer to keep warm. Continue pressing and cooking the tortillas in this fashion, adding them to the towel as they are made. Store leftovers for up to 2 weeks in a plastic bag in the refrigerator and reheat before serving.

notes

Using thin plastic is best, as it makes it easier to separate the dough from the bag, so avoid heavy-duty plastic storage bags.

How thick or thin you make your tortillas is up to you, but the most authentic thickness is between 1/16 and 1/8 inch (2 and 3 mm). When you're using your tortillas to make fried tacos, thinner is better.

At a very early age, my mom would bring me into the kitchen and say, "You have to pay attention and watch how I do things." Watching my *mamí* cook is like watching a professional. She moves with authority and finesse and knows her flavors through and through. When I was a kid, I would mimic the way her hands moved when she made tortillas before I even fully understood what I was doing.

My mom tells everyone how my first flour tortilla was shaped like the continent of Africa. I've come a long way, and I encourage you not to get discouraged with your first attempts. Being able to roll out a perfectly round flour tortilla is a hard-earned skill, so try to be patient. Just remember that it's not so much the shape of the tortilla but how it tastes. Spread a little butter on a just-made tortilla, take a bite, then you tell me if you care what shape that tortilla is!

flour tortillas

TORTILLAS DE HARINA

makes twelve to fourteen 10-inch (25-cm) tortillas

3 cups (375 g) all-purpose flour, plus more for dusting

1 teaspoon baking powder

1½ teaspoons salt

¾ cup (155 g) cold lard or vegetable shortening, plus more for greasing

1 cup (240 ml) hot water

✣ In a large bowl, whisk together the flour, baking powder, and salt. Add the lard or shortening and break it up with your hands until you have a cornmeal-like texture. Add the hot water and carefully mix with a spoon or your hands. You will have a very sticky dough. Remove the dough from the bowl onto a lightly floured surface and knead it for 5 to 8 minutes, dusting it with a small amount of flour as needed. Your dough will quickly turn from sticky to completely nonstick.

✣ Place the dough in a clean bowl, cover with plastic wrap or a damp towel, and allow it to rest for 5 minutes. While you wait, set a griddle or *comal* (tortilla griddle) over high heat.

✣ Spoon a dime-size amount of lard in the middle of your palm and rub it between your hands to grease them generously (the added grease will prevent the balls from sticking to each other). Take the dough out of the bowl and pinch some off with your index finger and thumb to form balls that are about 2 inches (5 cm) in diameter

(recipe continues on page 27)

(the balls should weigh about 2 ounces/55 g each). Set the dough balls on an even surface, greasing your hands every 2 or 3 balls.

⚹ Dust a work surface and rolling pin with flour. Create a small mound of flour on one of the top corners of your work surface. Press a dough ball into the flour mound, flattening it with your four fingers (rather than the tips of your fingers). Flip it and press it into the flour again.

⚹ Place the floured dough round at the center of your work surface and roll from the middle away from you and then back toward you. Flip the tortilla over so that the now oval-shaped tortilla is horizontal instead of vertical. Repeat the rolling motion and continue to roll and flip the tortilla in the same manner until it measures about 10 inches (25 cm) across and $\frac{1}{16}$ inch (2 mm) thick. Don't be scared of the dough—if you mess up, you have plenty more to work with, and if you break the dough, you can pinch it and roll over it to fix it with no problem. If at any point your rolling pin starts to get stuck, dust the tortilla surface and rolling pin lightly with flour and you will be all set to continue.

⚹ In one sweeping motion, almost as if you were going to brush the back of your hand over the griddle, gently lay your tortilla on the griddle, taking care not to burn yourself. Cook for 30 seconds, or until the tortilla bubbles up and lightly browns in spots. Flip the tortilla and cook for an additional 20 seconds on the second side. Flip the tortilla a third time and cook for an additional 15 seconds. Remove the tortilla from the griddle and wrap it in a kitchen towel or place it in a tortilla warmer to keep warm. Continue making tortillas and cooking them in this fashion, adding them to the towel as they are made.

salsas and cream sauces

SALSAS Y CREMAS

30 rustic mexican salsa

35 tomatillo salsa

37 cactus salsa

40 oaxacan avocado cream

42 chipotle cream sauce

44 roasted red pepper sauce

45 cilantro oil

When I think about the many regions of Mexico, I can name a number of salsas and sauces that come from each specific region, from the dark and smoky salsas of Oaxaca to the more vibrant and spicy red sauces of Guadalajara. No matter where you are in Mexico, one thing is certain—no meal is ever served without a delicious salsa or sauce to accompany it. While I could write a whole cookbook on just salsas and sauces, in this chapter I focus on some of my favorites and the most versatile ones—those that you can use with breakfast, lunch, and dinner dishes, as well as some with more complex and smoky flavors. Use these salsas to help elevate the flavor of your favorite dishes, even if it is just to remind yourself of the flavors you grew up with. *Provecho*.

Some of my fondest memories growing up are of my *mamí* cooking for us. The most amazing aromas would come out of that small kitchen, and they would envelop the house. Whenever I popped my head in, our *comal* (tortilla griddle) would be filled with vibrant tomatillos, bright red tomatoes, and different-colored chiles. We'd know it without asking when chiles de árbol were on the griddle to make her salsa, as our throats would immediately turn scratchy from the smoking chiles. To keep your chile smoke in check, make sure your kitchen is well ventilated and turn on the stove's vent hood if it has one.

rustic mexican salsa

SALSA RUSTICA MEXICANA

makes about 1½ cups (360 ml)

2 to 3 medium Roma tomatoes

1 jalapeño chile, stemmed

2 to 3 garlic cloves, peeled

2 to 4 whole chiles de árbol, stemmed

Salt

↳ Heat a medium skillet or *comal* (tortilla griddle) over low heat. Place the tomatoes, jalapeño, and garlic on the skillet and toast them until brown spots develop on the garlic but it does not become black, about 3 minutes. Remove the garlic from the pan. Continue roasting until the jalapeño and tomato skins blacken in places, the flesh begins to soften under the pressure of tongs, and the skin from the tomatoes starts to come away from the flesh (they will soften and begin to release their juices), about 20 minutes. If one ingredient starts to blacken before the others, remove it from the pan as needed.

↳ Heat a separate small skillet over low heat, add the chiles de árbol, and toast for 1 to 2 minutes, turning often, until they darken in color on both sides, taking care not to let them burn. The seeds will come out as you toast the chiles—you can use them or not depending on your heat preference.

↳ To prepare the salsa, begin by adding the garlic to a *molcajete* (mortar and pestle, see Notes) and mash until smooth. Add the chiles de árbol and break them up until a coarse red paste forms. Add the jalapeño and continue to mash until the mixture is fairly smooth but with some pieces remaining. You're looking for a rustic, chunky salsa, but make sure to break it up enough so no one gets an overly large piece of jalapeño. Last, add the tomatoes and mash them in carefully (they will be filled with hot steam) until they're just a little chunky but no large chunks remain. Season with salt and use a large spoon to mix and scrape down the sides of the *molcajete*. Serve the salsa in the *molcajete* or a decorative serving dish.

notes

If you don't have a *molcajete*, place all the ingredients in a food processor and pulse four or five times, until broken down but still chunky. Do not overblend—remember that it's not meant to be a smooth salsa.

See page 36 for more on spice levels and chile handling.

*rustic mexican salsa
(page 30)*

It's no secret that we are known for our salsas. While the most common salsas are tomato-based red salsas, there is nothing in the world quite like a tart and spicy *salsa verde* (green salsa). *Salsa verde* and tomatillo salsa are actually the same thing, as the green color comes from the green skin and flesh of the tomatillo.

This is our family's recipe for *salsa verde*. I use it in a number of dishes, from braised pork (see page 108) to Green Chilaquiles (page 154), or as a topping for tacos. You can adjust the heat level by reducing or increasing the number of chiles you include. But *cuidado* (careful)—the spiciness of the serranos and chiles de árbol may have you looking for the closest ice-cold beverage.

tomatillo salsa

SALSA VERDE

makes about 3 cups (720 mL)

12 ounces (340 g) fresh tomatillos

1 to 2 whole serrano chiles, stemmed

½ medium yellow onion, peeled

2 to 3 small garlic cloves, peeled

5 to 6 whole chiles de árbol, stemmed

Salt

❧ Peel the husks off the tomatillos and rinse them thoroughly under lukewarm water until their skin is smooth and they are no longer tacky or sticky.

❧ Place the tomatillos, serrano chiles, and onion in a large saucepan and add enough hot water to cover. Place over medium-high heat, bring to a simmer, then reduce the heat to medium-low and simmer until the tomatillos change color and just start to soften, about 5 minutes. Remove the ingredients from the pan using a slotted spoon and place them in blender along with the garlic. Reserve the cooking liquid.

❧ Meanwhile, heat a skillet or *comal* (tortilla griddle) over low heat. Add the chiles de árbol, and toast for 1 to 2 minutes, turning often, until they darken in color but don't burn. The seeds will come out as you toast the chiles—you can use them or not depending on your heat preference. What you are looking for is a darker, almost black, red color. Keep your windows open as you toast the chiles, as the fumes can affect the strangest parts of your throat and cause cough attacks for the family . . . *ahhh,* the memories.

(recipe continues)

⚡ Add the toasted chiles de árbol and seeds to the blender, pour in ¼ cup (60 ml) of the reserved tomatillo cooking liquid, and blend on medium-low speed until your desired consistency has been reached (see Notes). If your salsa is too thick, add more of the tomatillo cooking liquid.

⚡ Pour the salsa into a bowl and season with salt, starting with about 1 teaspoon and adjusting the amount as needed to balance the tartness of your tomatillos.

notes

The consistency of *salsa verde* varies depending on the dish you use it in. For Green Chilaquiles (page 154), make it a bit more on the liquidy side so your tortillas can soak up the salsa. For tacos, stick to a coarser and chunkier consistency to avoid a runny mess.

Keep in mind that chiles can vary in spice depending on the season, so you may want to cut off the edge of one of your chiles and taste it for heat. If it's too hot for your liking, remove the seeds and veins to turn the heat down. To turn up the heat, add more chiles.

Make sure not to touch your eyes after handling spicy chiles and wear gloves when working with them to protect your hands. The last thing you want is to start crying like a *novela* (soap opera) star.

When I was working on my finale menu, it was very important to me that it reflected my story. Essential to my story are my very humble beginnings, and nothing says humble like our Mexican custom of eating cactus. Cactus is not a delicacy by any means, but I am proud of my culture's ability to turn this unorthodox ingredient into so many beautiful and delicious recipes. Serve it on tacos or use it to dress your favorite dishes. No matter where you use it, it will add vibrant color and flavor to your meal.

The technique for salting cactus to remove slime from it and make it tender is one that I learned from my favorite Mexican chef, Enrique Olvera. I hope you enjoy this salsa—I know the *MasterChef* judges did!

cactus salsa

SALSA DE NOPAL

makes about 2 cups (480 ml)

2 cactus paddles

1 cup (240 g) coarse kosher salt

2 medium Roma tomatoes, chopped

½ medium red onion, finely chopped

1½ tablespoons fresh lime juice, or to taste

1 serrano chile, stemmed

Leaves from ½ bunch fresh cilantro, chopped

¼ teaspoon freshly ground black pepper

❧ If your cactus isn't already cleaned, clean it according to the directions on page 17 and cut it into ½-inch (12-mm) cubes.

❧ Place the cactus in a large bowl and add the salt. Toss until the cactus is fully covered and set aside to cure for 5 minutes; the cactus will begin to release slime. Turn it with a wooden spoon or spatula to make sure the salt reaches all of the pieces of cactus and allow to rest for an additional 2 to 3 minutes to release more slime. Remove the cactus from the bowl and place it in a strainer. Run it under cold water until all the visible salt has been removed. Taste the cactus for salt; it should be salty and have some give but should not taste raw. If it's too salty, rinse it some more. Pat dry with a paper towel.

❧ Move the cactus to a large bowl and add the tomatoes, onion, and lime juice and toss with a spoon or spatula. Slice the chile in half lengthwise and remove the seeds and veins if you want to keep the heat down. Thinly slice each half widthwise to create half-moon slices and add them to the bowl.

❧ Add the cilantro and fold until completely incorporated. Stir in the pepper and taste. If it's too salty, add a bit more lime juice for additional acidity.

*cactus salsa
(page 37)*

I remember the first time I *really* tasted an avocado. I was about six years old and we were sitting down to eat tacos at my *abuelita*'s (grandmother's) house in Tijuana. My grandmother had arranged some avocado slices into a simple carne asada taco. I stared down at it and thought, "What is that?" Sensing my uncertainty, she yelled, "*Cometelo!* (Eat it!)" I was so scared I picked up my taco and took a huge bite.

I turned to my abuelita and said, "Oh, it tastes like guacamole!" (in Spanish, of course). She laughed as I let this new information sink in. I took another big bite and enjoyed the flavor of that creamy avocado dancing in my mouth.

This recipe melds the creamy deliciousness of Hass avocado with Mexican sour cream. It is bright and ultra-creamy, and it is the perfect finish to any taco, burrito, quesadilla, or whatever your heart desires! Go ahead . . . *Cometelo!*

oaxacan avocado cream

CREMA DE AGUACATE OAXAQUEÑA

makes about 1½ cups (360 ml)

1 large ripe Hass avocado

½ cup (120 ml) Oaxacan sour cream (see Notes) or crème fraîche

1½ tablespoons fresh lime juice

Salt

❖ Using a 6-inch (15-cm) knife, *carefully* slice through the stem end of the avocado until you can feel the pit. Proceed to run your knife down one side following the pit, but don't press too eagerly. A ripe avocado will be very easy to cut, so don't exert yourself or you can risk a cut. Continue cutting all the way around the pit until you reach the original cut.

❖ Set your knife down, hold each side of the avocado in your hands, and twist in opposite directions. Carefully remove the pit of the avocado either with a spoon or fork. (If your avocado isn't ripe enough, this may prove difficult; if so, stab your knife into the pit and twist in order to remove it. If you are unable to remove the pit, use another avocado, as this avocado is not ripe and will taste too earthy.)

❖ Run a large spoon along the inside of the skin of the avocado to remove the flesh from the skin. Don't worry how perfectly the avocado comes out, as you are going to be pureeing it anyway!

※ In a small blender or food processor (a mini food processor works well), combine the avocado flesh, sour cream, and lime juice, and blend until smooth. If your avocado is not ripe enough or the sour cream is too thick, add a tablespoon or so of water to get things moving in the machine, but make sure to keep the consistency thick and mousse-like (see Notes). Remove from the blender and season with salt.

※ Fit a piping bag with a small circular tip and add the avocado cream to the bag or spoon the cream into a squeeze bottle. To plate with tamales or tacos, place your point close to the plate, squeeze out a little cream, and lift the tip straight up. This will make your dollop look like the perfect kiss! Because avocados are finicky and will turn brown and dull, this *crema* will not keep longer than 4 hours, even when stored in an airtight container. So put it on everything and be generous with it!

notes

Oaxacan sour cream is denser than typical sour cream and is salted and textured much like a crème fraîche. If you cannot find it, use crème fraîche or, in a pinch, regular sour cream and a bit more salt to achieve a similar balance of flavor.

Err on the side of thicker (but not chunky) than thinner for your avocado cream, because if it is too thin, you will have a dripping mess that cannot be piped.

One of my mom's favorite flavors to experiment with is, by far, chipotle. She would make us the most delicious plates using this chile's smoky and spicy flavor profile, turning a dish as simple as meatballs into something mind-blowing.

Chipotle crema has been done a great many ways. In coming up with my version of it, I incorporated everything I've learned about building flavor in salsa. Some of those ingredients are not common in *chipotle cremas*, but I assure you, each one of them will make this spectacular sauce your new staple!

This sauce is perfect with my Mexican Cordon Bleu (page 100) and Sautéed Chayote and Red Cabbage (page 135); it can also be served with Green Chilaquiles (page 154), enchiladas, eggs, and any number of meat dishes—the sky is really the limit, but always serve it warm, as this is different from chipotle sour cream (see page 102), which is served cold and used as a garnish.

chipotle cream sauce

CHIPOTLE CREMA

makes about 1¾ cups (420 ml)

1 tablespoon canola oil

¼ medium white onion, minced

2 garlic cloves, minced

1 teaspoon dried Mexican oregano

1 small tomato, chopped

1 cup (240 ml) heavy cream

1 to 2 canned chipotle chiles in adobo sauce

Salt

⋙ Heat the oil in a medium sauté pan over medium heat. Add the onion and cook for 30 seconds, or until fragrant. Add the garlic and oregano and cook for an additional 30 seconds, or until the garlic starts to soften. Add the tomato and sauté until softened, about 2 minutes. Reduce the heat to low, carefully pour in the cream, and bring to a simmer. Immediately remove from the heat.

⋙ A little bit goes a long way with smoky chipotle chiles, so if you have never worked with them, start with one, and then add another if you want to turn up the heat. Place the chile in a blender, carefully pour in the hot cream mixture, and blend on medium speed for about 1 minute, until smooth and bright orange in color. Taste for salt and season accordingly; if the sauce is not spicy enough for you, add an additional chile and blend again until smooth. This is a dairy-based cream sauce that will keep a maximum of 3 to 4 days in the fridge, so use it quickly.

roasted red
pepper sauce
(page 44)

oaxacan
avocado cream
(page 40)

chipotle
cream sauce
(opposite)

cilantro oil
(page 45)

I had to include this sauce in this book because it was the one that helped me win my first team challenge of the season, breaking the ever-dreaded Claudia curse! It is based on a veal demi-glace I was working on and a roasted red pepper sauce I like to make. The combo was a complete hit with the ranchers and cowboys that day, and I hope it's a hit in your household too. *Yee-haw!*

roasted red pepper sauce

SALSA DE CHILE TATEMADO

makes about 2½ cups (600 ml)

2 medium Roma tomatoes

1 jalapeño chile

1 pound (455 g) fresh piquillo peppers, roasted, or 1 (14-ounce/400-g) can roasted piquillo peppers, drained

4 garlic cloves, peeled

1 small yellow onion, quartered

½ cup (120 ml) beef stock or veal demi-glace, plus more if needed

4 sprigs fresh thyme, tied with kitchen string

Salt and freshly ground black pepper

Cayenne pepper (optional)

⚜ Heat a skillet or *comal* (tortilla griddle) over medium-low heat. Place the tomatoes and jalapeño on the skillet and heat until the tomatoes are almost completely darkened on all sides, softened, and releasing their juices and the jalapeño is fragrant and blistered. Remove the stem and cut the jalapeño in half. Remove the seeds using a spoon if you'd like your sauce on the milder side.

⚜ In a blender, combine the tomatoes, jalapeño, piquillo peppers, garlic, onion, and stock, and blend until smooth. Pour the mixture into a medium saucepan. Add the thyme and season with salt and pepper. Place over low heat and bring to a simmer, adding a little more stock if it's too thick.

⚜ Once it simmers, remove the thyme, taste for heat, and add a little cayenne if needed. The sauce will keep in an airtight container in the refrigerator for 5 to 7 days. Bring it to a boil before serving.

I learned so many amazing things in the *MasterChef* kitchen. Being able to create infused oils is one of the skills I am most grateful for, and this cilantro oil adds flavor and color to so many dishes, from the simplest of plates to the creamiest of soups. It's like the Mexican version of Italian herb oil. We used this oil during the Vegetarian Team Challenge, and while our dish wasn't a winner that night, this oil is a winner any time.

cilantro oil

ACEITE DE CILANTRO

makes about 1¼ cups (300 ml)

2 large bunches fresh cilantro

1¼ cups (300 ml) canola oil

Salt

» Start by cutting 1 inch (2.5 cm) from the thick ends of the cilantro stems. Chop the leaves and tender stems (stop about 1 inch/2.5 cm from the bottom of the cut stems) until you have 2 packed cups (80 g). Save any remaining cilantro for another recipe. Place the cilantro in the blender with ¼ cup (60 ml) of the oil.

» Blend on low speed, slowly drizzling in the remaining oil through the hole in the top of the blender. Do not overblend or blend on high speed, as this can cook the cilantro and turn it a dark green or brown color. Season with salt and pulse until incorporated.

» Line a fine-mesh sieve or *chinois* with a double layer of cheesecloth. Pour the blended oil into the sieve and, using a large rubber spatula, push the oil mixture through the sieve into a large bowl, pressing on it with the spatula to get out all the flavored oil. Discard the cilantro pulp.

» Pour the oil through a funnel into a squeeze bottle for ease of plating. It will keep, refrigerated, for up to 5 days.

mazatlán-style seafood

MARISCOS ESTILO MAZATLÁN

When I started to think about which recipes I wanted to include in my book, my first idea was that I wanted to share with you a bit of where my family comes from, *un pedacito de mi Mazatlán* (a little piece of my Mazatlán).

One of the main reasons I cook the way I do is that the recipes I use have been handed down through several generations of powerful women. In fact, in the little town of Barron, which borders the largest river in Mazatlán, the town folk still tell stories of the women I am proud to call my ancestors. Women like my great-grandmother Julia, *una gran señora* (a grand woman) who would cook from the wee hours of the morning to feed the men who worked the fishing boats til well past sunset and the workers tending the nearby mango or chile crops.

This is an homage to a region of Mexico so often overlooked for its gastronomy, a cuisine based on fresh seafood elevated with some of the most basic of ingredients. And it's a tribute to all of the hardworking men and women who live in Mazatlán and earn their living with honor. *Por ustedes!*

When Father's Day rolls around, I'll turn to my dad and ask him what he'd like me to make for his special meal. I don't really have to ask, though, because the answer is always *aguachile*.

Aguachile translates to "chile water," and the dish is named for the spicy acidic liquid in which these shrimp are cooked.

Although there are many different versions of *aguachile*, we typically make this dish with habanero chiles. I realize that most palates cannot handle that level of spice, so I've called for chiles de árbol or serranos instead. However, if you are a serious fan of heat, feel free to turn it up by swapping in super spicy habaneros.

spicy shrimp ceviche

AGUACHILE

serves 6

2 pounds (910 g) medium or large shrimp, peeled

1 teaspoon salt

1 cup (240 ml) fresh lime juice

2 fresh chiles de árbol or 1 to 3 fresh serrano chiles, stemmed

1 red onion, thinly sliced into half moons

1 large cucumber, thinly sliced into half moons

1 large Roma tomato, sliced into half moons

Up to 1 teaspoon crushed red pepper flakes (optional)

» Butterfly the shrimp: On a cutting board, place each shrimp on its side and insert a knife about three-quarters of the way into the outside curve of the shrimp from the head to the tail, making sure not to cut all the way through. Remove the vein with the tip of your knife.

» Place the butterflied shrimp in a large nonmetallic bowl, toss with the salt, and refrigerate while you make the sauce.

» In a blender, combine the lime juice and whole chiles and blend until the chiles are completely broken down. Add the onion slices and half of the cucumber slices to the shrimp and toss, coating the onion and cucumber with salt.

» Line a platter with the remaining cucumber slices and all of the tomato slices. Spread the shrimp mixture into a single layer on the platter using a nonmetallic spoon or spatula and slowly pour the chile-lime sauce over the shrimp (see Notes). Sprinkle with the red pepper flakes, if using. I hope you have a cold drink nearby, because you're going to need it!

notes

In Mazatlán, *aguachile* is served up right after it's made—raw. If you'd like your shrimp to cook in the lime juice a bit, cover it before garnishing and put it in the refrigerator for about 10 minutes, mixing it once or twice, before serving. You will know the shrimp is thoroughly cooked when it turns pinkish white and you no longer see any gray.

Every other Sunday, I find myself calling my friends Tania and Eiliana in search of *mariscos* (seafood). When we aren't making them at home, we'll visit our favorite food truck and chow down on some *almejas preparadas* (clam ceviche).

Clams can take some effort to pry open; you'll just need to be patient and stern with them. It's worth the work, though, as preparing them ceviche style makes for one of the most authentic, delicious, and regenerative dishes you can feed yourself.

clam ceviche in the shell

ALMEJAS PREPARADAS EN CONCHA

serves 4

4 large live clams

2 tablespoons fresh lime juice

¼ cup (60 ml) tomato juice cocktail such as Clamato

¼ cup chopped tomato

¼ medium cucumber, peeled and chopped

2 tablespoons chopped yellow onion

2 tablespoons chopped fresh cilantro

1 jalapeño or serrano chile, minced (optional)

Salt and freshly ground black pepper

Bottled hot sauce (optional)

⊁ Scrub the clam shells well. Take a shucking knife and place it in the small separation between the edges of a clam by the hinge.

⊁ Place the clam in one hand, using a towel to cushion your hand for extra safety. Using your other hand, slowly but firmly rock the knife back and forth to ease it into the sides of the shell, pushing your palm against the knife for traction. This will take some effort. Be *very* careful. If you cannot identify where your knife is going, use the back of the knife to scrape off some of the lip of the shell so you are able to see the closure.

⊁ Once you have wedged the knife in between the top and bottom shells, push firmly toward the top of the shell, running the knife across the top and cutting at the two abductor muscles holding it together. You want to reach as far back as the valve, but do not cut through. Do this quickly. Use your knife to open the shell enough so you can place your fingers inside and pry the mollusk open without breaking the valve. Cut the two other abductor muscles and place the clam meat along with its juices into a small bowl. Reserve the clam shells. Repeat with the other clams.

⊁ Roughly chop the clam meat, then return it to the bowl with its juices. Add the lime juice and allow the clam meat to marinate for about 2 minutes, then add the tomato cocktail, tomato, cucumber, onion, cilantro, and chile, if using. Season with salt and pepper and mix to combine.

⊁ Spoon the ceviche into the shells and serve with a bottled hot sauce, if desired, and ice-cold *cerveza* (beer).

Growing up, my *abuelita* (grandmother) would share stories about my great-grandma Julia's beachside pop-up restaurant; every day local fishermen would bring her buckets of fresh mussels that she'd prepare, with tourists and locals swooning for the grilled treats.

In my take on grilled mussels, the smokiness of the grill and the savory juices of the mussels, mixed with all that amazing garlic, will have your mouth watering instantly. Munchkin is also a big fan of these mussels, as they are by far her favorite form of seafood. Like mother, like daughter!

grilled mussels

CHORROS AL CARBON

serves 8

1 cup (2 sticks/225 g) salted butter

8 to 10 garlic cloves, minced

4 pounds (1.8 kg) fresh mussels, scrubbed and debearded

Leaves from ½ bunch fresh cilantro, chopped

4 to 6 limes, cut into wedges

Hot sauce of choice

⟫ Preheat an outdoor grill to medium-high heat (about 375°F/190°C). Mesquite or real wood will add that authentic smokiness to your mussels, but an electric grill will work as well.

⟫ In a medium saucepan, melt the butter over low heat. Add the garlic and immediately turn the heat off.

⟫ Place the mussels in a disposable aluminum roasting pan, pour the butter over the mussels, and toss with a spoon to coat the mussels in the butter.

⟫ Place the mussels on the grill, cover with the lid or aluminum foil, and allow to smoke for 3 minutes. Uncover and mix the mussels again (some mussels will begin to open). Cover again and grill for another 3 minutes, then toss again and cook for another 3 minutes. The amount of liquid inside your roasting pan will increase as the mussels begin to open. After your third check, all of the mussels should be open and perfectly smoked; if not, give it another round, then discard any that haven't opened. Remove from the heat.

⟫ Sprinkle with the cilantro and squeeze a couple of limes over the mussels. Serve immediately, with more lime wedges and hot sauce alongside.

No, this recipe isn't named after any of my home state of California's famous governors! It's actually named after a governor of the state of Sinaloa who once visited the city of Culiacán. A local chef invented a taco to welcome the governor, and when he asked what the taco was called, the chef named it the "governor taco." These sautéed shrimp tacos went on to become a crowd favorite across port towns all over Mexico.

This recipe calls for a sauce called Salsa Maggi. It's like a Mexican version of soy sauce, and I use it in several recipes in the book. Start off slow and add as much or as little as you like to suit your taste.

governor tacos (sautéed shrimp tacos)

TACOS GOBERNADOR

makes 8 tacos

8 (6-inch/15-cm) corn tortillas, homemade (see page 20) or store-bought

8 ounces (225 g) Oaxaca cheese or Monterey Jack cheese, pulled or cut into thin strips

1 tablespoon canola oil

1 pound (455 g) small to medium shrimp, peeled and deveined

Salt and freshly ground black pepper

1 small red onion, thinly sliced

1 medium green bell pepper, cored, seeded, and thinly sliced

¼ cup (60 ml) Maggi sauce

» Preheat a griddle or *comal* (tortilla griddle) over medium-high heat to get it nice and hot.

» Reduce the heat under the griddle to low, add a couple of tortillas, and heat them for 15 to 30 seconds on each side, until soft and malleable. Add 1 ounce (28 g) of cheese to one side of each tortilla and fold the empty side over the cheese side to form a quesadilla. Press down on the quesadilla with a metal spatula for the first few seconds so the cheese sticks, then cook for 1 to 2 minutes on each side, until the cheese is completely melted and the tortillas start to get crisp. Repeat with the remaining tortillas and cheese.

» Heat the oil in a large skillet over high heat. Add the shrimp and season lightly with salt and pepper. Cook until just turning pink on both sides, 2 to 4 minutes, flipping the shrimp halfway through cooking. Remove the shrimp to a bowl. Add the onion and bell pepper to the pan and cook until crisp-tender, about 3 minutes, stirring often. Return the shrimp to the pan, add the Maggi sauce, and toss quickly until incorporated and the shrimp are fully cooked through.

» To serve, open up a crispy quesadilla and add some shrimp and vegetables. Fold it back over and serve piping hot.

So much of my *MasterChef* journey was about reinventing dishes I grew up with. I remember losing sleep trying to come up with ways to elevate the most rustic of dishes. This grilled octopus, which I made during the "Top 3 Challenge," is one I am particularly proud of; nevertheless, it was judged as too rustic for the *MasterChef* kitchen. The plating pictured here was inspired by my friend and colleague Chef Iker Castillo, who consistently pushes me and inspires me to do greater things because he, too, aims to elevate Mexican food as we know it. We should all be so lucky to have people like him in our circles. Thanks, Dude.

Serve the octopus over Oaxacan Avocado Cream (page 40) and pineapple-mango salsa (see page 102) or with Frisée and Poblano Salad with Honey-Citrus-Jalapeño Dressing (page 130) like I did on the show. No matter which you choose, the dish will be delicious!

grilled achiote octopus

PULPO ACHIOTE ASADO

serves 4

FOR THE ACHIOTE OCTOPUS:

2 fresh octopi (2 to 3 pounds/ 910 g to 1.4 kg each)

2 cups (480 g) coarse kosher salt

1 tablespoon annatto seeds

8 garlic cloves

2 tablespoons dried Mexican oregano

(ingredients continue)

TO MAKE THE OCTOPUS:

❧ Pull back the tentacles of each octopus, push the head of the octopus inward, and remove the beak using a pinching motion with two fingers to push it out.

❧ Place a dish towel over a large cutting board or flat work surface. Place one octopus over the towel and cover with 1 cup (240 g) of the salt. Place another towel over the octopus to cover it and prevent splatter. Using a French rolling pin (the kind without handles) or another sturdy wooden object (not a meat tenderizer, as they are too heavy and will break the tentacles), hit the octopus a number of times to tenderize it. Take care not to hit the tentacles too hard, as they can break. Thoroughly rinse off the salt and set aside. Repeat with the second octopus.

❧ Bring a large pot of water to a soft (not rolling) boil. Add the annatto seeds, garlic, and oregano. Invert the head of an octopus so that it is easy to hold. Hold it high up over the pot, dip the tentacles into the

(recipe continues)

FOR THE ACHIOTE GLAZE:

1 orange, juiced

2 tablespoons achiote paste

1 tablespoon red wine vinegar

1 teaspoon sugar

⅛ teaspoon salt

Cooking spray

Fresh micro cilantro, for garnish

Sliced red radishes, for garnish

water for 10 seconds, and pull them out. Keep it out of the water for about 10 seconds, then plunge it back again, this time holding the tentacles in the water for about 15 seconds. Pull the octopus back out of the water and place it in a bowl while you repeat with the second octopus. Drop both of the whole octopi back in to the pot (see Notes). Bring to a simmer, cover the pot, and cook at a low simmer for about 1 hour, until the octopi are fork-tender. Remove the octopi from the water. Cut the tentacles from the heads, slice the heads into rounds, and set aside.

TO MAKE THE ACHIOTE GLAZE:

» Pour the orange juice into a small saucepan and add the achiote paste, vinegar, sugar, and salt. Bring to a simmer over low heat and cook until the sugar and achiote paste are completely dissolved and the mixture is thick. Set aside to cool.

TO FINISH THE DISH:

» Set a grill pan over medium-high heat and spray it generously with cooking spray.

» In a large bowl, toss the octopus pieces with the achiote glaze to fully coat. Place them on the grill pan in a single layer and grill until just charred, 30 seconds to 1 minute on each side; remove from the heat. To plate, spoon some avocado cream or frisée salad over four plates. Create small mounds of octopus on top, beginning first with the head and finishing with the tentacles, and serve, garnished with the micro cilantro and radishes.

notes

Dipping the octopus tentacles in the boiling water twice breaks the fibers so it doesn't toughen up as it cooks.

You can reduce the cooking time to about 30 minutes by using a pressure cooker to cook the octopus like I did on the show.

My signature *MasterChef* dish had to be something that represented me. After all, it would be how I earned my apron and a place in the competition. It needed to be—as Chef Ramsay put it—me on a plate. I wanted to go with something traditional but technically difficult, which is how I came to choose head-on, shell-on shrimp as the focus of the dish. They are very easy to overcook, so follow my instructions carefully and you will not only have a beautifully cooked meal, but a dish worthy of the praise of family and friends.

The grape pico salsa was an untraditional but tasty pairing, providing a punch of sweet acidity to the salty, garlicky shrimp to balance out the dish. To serve your shrimp Mazatlán style, use Mexican White Rice (page 142) as an accompaniment.

garlic-sautéed head-on shrimp with grape pico salsa

CAMARONES BARBONES AL MOJO DE AJO CON SALSA BANDERA DE UVA

serves 4

FOR THE GRAPE PICO SALSA:

1½ cups (225 g) chopped red grapes

½ small red onion, minced

¼ cup (10 g) finely chopped fresh cilantro leaves

½ serrano chile, minced

1 tablespoon fresh lime juice, or to taste

Salt and freshly ground black pepper

(ingredients continue)

TO MAKE THE PICO SALSA:

⚜ Place the grapes, onion, cilantro, chile, and lime juice in a medium bowl and toss to combine. Season with salt and pepper. Set aside while you cook the shrimp.

TO MAKE THE SHRIMP:

⚜ Melt 2 tablespoons of the butter in a large skillet over medium heat. Add one-quarter of the minced garlic and cook for 20 seconds. Add three of the shrimp to the pan on their sides and season each shrimp with a pinch of salt. Cook, keeping the garlic butter at a simmer and lowering the heat if the garlic starts to brown too fast, until the shrimp begin to take on color, about 2 minutes. Flip the shrimp over and tilt the pan, using a large spoon to baste the shrimp with the garlic butter sauce. Cook, continuing to baste, for an additional 2 minutes, or until the flesh of the shrimp begins to just pull away from the shell (see Notes, page 60). Remove the shrimp from the pan and place on a platter.

(recipe continues)

FOR THE SHRIMP

½ cup (1 stick/115 g) salted butter, divided

8 garlic cloves, minced, divided

12 large head-on shrimp or prawns

Salt

✤ Remove the garlic butter from the pan to a bowl and repeat with the remaining butter, garlic, and shrimp, adding the finished shrimp to the platter as they are done. Garnish with the grape pico salsa and Mexican White Rice (page 142) if you like.

notes

The residual steam in the shells will continue to cook the shrimp after you remove them from the pan. Keeping them from getting over-cooked is something that takes practice, so check your first batch and adjust the timing as needed. Watching for the shrimp to pull away from the shell is the most reliable indicator of doneness for shell-on shrimp.

You all met my mother in the *MasterChef* "Family Reunion" episode. My mom was absolutely thrilled to be served dinner by all three chefs—Gordon Ramsay, Graham Elliot, and Christina Tosi. She still boasts about it! Something you should know about my mother—other than the fact that she is a better cook than I am—is that she absolutely loves this dish. Growing up, my mom wanted nothing more than a 3-pound fish all to herself for her birthday dinner!

While this technique may be unfamiliar to some of you, believe me, there is something absolutely magical about grilling a fish whole and eating it family style with grilled refried bean taquitos (see page 144) on the side.

Warm some tortillas (see page 20 or 22) to eat with this flaky fish, and if you really want to be transported to Mexico, grab yourself a crisp cold beer. You'll see just how perfect this summer favorite is.

grilled red snapper

PESCADO PARGO ZARANDEADO

serves 4

FOR THE FISH:

1 tablespoon mayonnaise

1½ teaspoons yellow mustard

4 garlic cloves, minced

½ teaspoon New Mexico chile powder

¼ cup (60 ml) Maggi sauce, divided

1 (3- to 4-pound/1.4- to 1.8-kg) red snapper, butterflied from head to tail (ask your fishmonger to do this for you)

Salt and freshly ground black pepper

Cooking spray

(ingredients continue)

TO MAKE THE FISH:

⚜ Preheat an outdoor grill to medium heat.

⚜ In a medium bowl, whisk together the mayonnaise, mustard, garlic, chile powder, and 1 tablespoon of the Maggi sauce until incorporated.

⚜ Place a large piece of aluminum foil (large enough to hold your butterflied fish completely open) on a work surface. If your fish still has its fins, you can cut them so your fish lies completely flat. Place the fish on the foil skin-side down. Season the flesh side generously with salt and pepper, then generously brush the flesh with the seasoned mayonnaise. (There is no need to brush the marinade on the skin, as it won't be eaten.)

⚜ Spray a large fish-grilling cage with cooking spray on the side that will be touching the flesh side of the fish. Using the aluminum foil as an aid, place the fish onto the grilling cage and close it. Flip it over so the flesh side is the first to hit the grill. Discard the foil.

⚜ Sear the fish until it starts to cook through and you have some crispy, almost burnt pieces of fish, 3 to 5 minutes. Flip the fish so the

(recipe continues)

FOR THE VEGETABLES:

1 teaspoon canola oil

1 medium red onion, sliced into thin half-moons

1 medium green bell pepper, seeded and sliced ¼ inch (6 mm) thick

1 large tomato, sliced

Lime wedges

skin side is facing down and grill until the fish is cooked through, 7 to 10 minutes more.

TO MAKE THE VEGETABLES:

➤ Heat the oil in a medium sauté pan over high heat. Add the onion and bell pepper and cook for 1 to 2 minutes, until starting to soften. Add the remaining 3 tablespoons of Maggi sauce and continue to cook until the onion begins to wilt slightly. Remove from the heat.

➤ To plate, very carefully remove the fish from the cage and place it on a large serving platter, skin-side down. Garnish with the sautéed onion and pepper and the tomato slices. The heat of the fish will warm the tomatoes slightly but not cook them. Serve with lime wedges alongside.

main dishes

PLATILLOS FUERTES

In Mexico, like many other countries, main dishes usually aren't accompanied by carbohydrate or vegetable sides to make them a complete meal. Unlike American or French plating, Mexican main dishes like tamales or *birria*, a slow-braised beef dish, can stand on their own and don't need any sides. I have included many of these types of recipes in this chapter to share a true taste of Mexico. I wanted to show you why I couldn't back down from the amazing flavors of the Mexican kitchen during my time in the *MasterChef* kitchen.

No matter how you serve your dishes, you will absolutely love the depth of flavor you can achieve with the recipes in this chapter. It is the longest chapter in this book, and it will offer you many different choices and options, no matter what you are in the mood for. Many of my fans have asked for vegetarian, vegan, and gluten-free recipes. I have taken care to sprinkle them throughout this chapter and the rest of the book so you can see how Mexican food offers many options for a variety of ways of eating (please check the Notes section of each recipe for variations). My hope is that however you eat, you will fall in love with Mexican food!

When I first walked into the *MasterChef* kitchen, one of the executive producers, Adeline Ramage Rooney, said to me, "If you were to go on and win this I would love to see *chiles relleños* in your cookbook!" I am dedicating this recipe to her. Adeline, one day I hope to have the privilege of making them for you personally.

When you decide to make *chiles relleños*, I've got your back. There's a reason I've illustrated the process for you here. Simply put, it takes a number of steps to get these chiles done! If you've never made this dish before, just remember—the results are not always pretty, but they will always taste amazing. Sometimes real food isn't pretty, and this is a *real* recipe. There's no fluff here—well, except for the fluffy egg whites! (Sorry, I couldn't help myself . . .) Serve with Mexican Red Rice (page 140) and Traditional Refried Beans (page 143) for a complete meal.

stuffed poblano chiles

CHILES RELLEÑOS

makes 6 stuffed chiles

6 large poblano chiles

12 ounces (340 g) queso fresco or Monterey Jack cheese, cut into 1-ounce (28-g) pieces

¼ cup plus 1 tablespoon (40 g) all-purpose flour, divided

Canola oil, for frying

5 large eggs, separated

½ medium yellow onion, thinly sliced

4 garlic cloves, minced

(ingredients continue on page 72)

TO ROAST THE CHILES:

✣ Turn a burner to the highest setting and place a chile directly on the flame (you can use multiple burners to roast more than one chile at a time). Turn them often with tongs until the skin is blackened all over. Make sure to keep the heat very high because you don't want to cook the flesh too much, or it will become too soft and difficult to keep intact. The chiles will snap and crackle as the skin blisters, but don't be scared; just keep turning them until the skin blackens and pulls away from the flesh. Place the chiles in an airtight bag and cover with a kitchen towel to help the chiles sweat for 5 to 10 minutes (this will lock in the steam and allow the skin to separate from the flesh). Remove them from the bag carefully, as some steam may come out.

✣ Using a large paper towel, remove the fire-roasted skin, leaving the gorgeous green flesh; do this carefully so as not to tear the chiles. If you are having a hard time removing the skin, use your fingers. If there are any unroasted pieces of skin remaining, just leave them on. I assure you no one will notice!

(recipe continues on page 72)

5 medium Roma tomatoes,
2 chopped and 3 blended into
a puree

3 cups (720 ml) vegetable
stock, chicken stock, or water,
plus more if needed

Salt and freshly ground black
pepper

》 Carefully make a small slit on the side of each chile and stuff each one with 2 ounces (55 g) of cheese. Place them on a plate and set aside to air-dry for a few minutes (this assures that the dredge will take hold of the chiles). Using a small sieve, dust the chiles lightly with ¼ cup (30 g) of the flour, until they are completely covered, flipping them back and forth carefully as you dust them (don't roll them in a vat of flour, as too much flour can cause your egg dredge to fall off).

》 Pour about 1½ inches (4 cm) of oil into a large skillet over medium-high heat and bring it to 350°F (175°C).

》 In a large bowl, beat the egg whites at high speed until semi-firm peaks form. Add the egg yolks and beat until just incorporated. Sprinkle in the remaining 1 tablespoon of flour and beat until incorporated. Do not overbeat; you want to keep them fluffy.

》 Working with one chile at a time, hold the chile by its stem, dip it into the egg mixture, covering every part of the chile but the stem (use a spoon to help you, see Notes), and carefully place the chile in the hot oil. The oil will fizzle, not spit at you, if it's at the correct temperature. If the oil starts to spit at any time, turn the heat down a bit. Using a metal spoon, gently scoop the oil over the chile as it cooks. Cook for about 3 minutes, until the egg is light golden brown on the top. Remove the chile from the oil using a slotted spoon and place it on a paper towel–lined plate. Continue until all the chiles have been fried.

⁂ Heat 1 tablespoon of your frying oil in a separate large skillet or shallow pot over medium heat. Add the onion and sauté for 1 minute, or until it starts to soften, then add the garlic and cook until it's aromatic and lightly browned, another minute or two. Add the chopped tomatoes and cook for another 2 minutes, or until they begin to soften. Add the pureed tomatoes, bring to a simmer, and simmer for 2 minutes, then add the stock and season with salt and pepper.

⁂ Bring to a boil, then reduce the heat and simmer for 10 minutes. You're looking for a thin broth rather than a tomato sauce consistency. Add more stock or water at the end of the 10 minutes if needed. Taste and adjust the seasoning as needed. Gently place the chiles in the broth (they should be three quarters covered by the broth), return to a gentle simmer, cover, and simmer for 7 minutes. Turn off the heat, allow the chiles to rest for 5 minutes (this ensures that the cheese fully melts and the broth will slightly thicken), and then serve.

notes

To keep this dish vegetarian, use vegetable stock rather than chicken stock.

The egg needs to fully coat the chiles so when you fry them the egg expands and puffs; if it's not fully covered, you run the risk of the chile exploding.

Use any remaining egg mixture to fry up egg patties for the kids.

Working closely in the competition with Hetal, a vegetarian, made me take a look at what Mexican cooking had to offer in the way of meatless dishes. I wanted to include several of those recipes in this book so people would know that we Mexicans have a number of excellent vegetarian dishes.

When I shared this dish with Hetal, she was blown away, because, as she said, she could taste the love. I hope that you can taste it too! Serve with Mexican Red Rice (page 140) and Traditional Refried Beans (page 143) for a complete meal.

cauliflower fritters

TORTITAS DE COLIFLOR

serves 4 to 6

1 medium head cauliflower

Canola oil, for frying

4 large eggs, separated

½ small onion, sliced

3 garlic cloves, minced

4 medium Roma tomatoes, 2 chopped and 2 blended into a puree (see Notes)

2 cups (480 ml) vegetable stock, chicken stock, or water

Salt and freshly ground black pepper

⌁ Cut the cauliflower into medium florets; try to keep them all the same size. If any florets are very large, carefully cut them in half, keeping the florets as intact as possible.

⌁ Bring a large pot of water to a boil over high heat.

⌁ Blanch the florets for 2 to 3 minutes, until they change from bright white to off-white but aren't cooked through (this ensures that your cauliflower cooks through later). Pour them into a colander and leave to drain completely.

⌁ Pour about 1 inch (2.5 cm) of oil into a large skillet over medium heat; bring it to 350°F (175°C).

⌁ In a large bowl, using an electric mixer, beat the egg whites on high speed until semi-firm peaks form. Add the yolks and beat until just incorporated. Do not overbeat the eggs; you want to keep them fluffy.

⌁ Working in batches, dip each floret individually into the egg mixture, covering them completely (yes, even covering part of your fingers—see Notes), and carefully place them in the hot oil. The oil will fizzle, not spit at you, if it's at the correct temperature. If the oil starts to spit at any time, turn the heat down a bit. Using a metal spoon, gently scoop the oil over the cauliflower as it cooks. Cook for about 3 minutes, until the egg is lightly golden brown on top. Remove the florets from the oil using a slotted spoon and place them on a paper towel–lined plate. Continue until all the florets have been fried.

✷ Heat 1 tablespoon of your frying oil in a separate large skillet or shallow pot over medium heat. Add the onion and sauté for 1 minute, or until starting to soften, then add the garlic and cook until it's aromatic and lightly browned, another 2 minutes or so. Add the chopped tomatoes and cook for another 2 minutes, or until they begin to soften. Add the pureed tomatoes, bring to a simmer, and simmer for 2 minutes, then add the stock and season with salt and pepper.

✷ Bring to a boil, then reduce the heat and simmer for 10 minutes (you're looking for a thin broth rather than a sauce consistency). Taste and adjust the seasoning as needed. Gently place the cauliflower in the broth, return to a low simmer, cover, and simmer for 8 to 10 minutes, until the florets are fork-tender and the broth is slightly thickened. Allow the cauliflower to rest for 5 minutes before serving.

notes

If fresh tomatoes aren't available, you can substitute one 8-ounce (230-g) can of tomatoes.

To keep this dish vegetarian, use vegetable stock rather than chicken stock.

The egg needs to fully coat the cauliflower so when you fry the cauliflower the egg expands and puffs.

Use any remaining egg mixture to fry up egg patties for the kids or anyone who doesn't like cauliflower.

Growing up with a single mom meant at times we didn't have much, but our bellies were always full and warm, as there were always *frijoles* (beans) and corn masa in our house. This recipe brings me back to those times. I hope you can taste the love in these simple yet delicious dumplings.

This is a great recipe to involve the children in, as their little fingers make the perfect indentations the masa balls need to cook through evenly.

corn dumplings in pinto bean cream

CHOCHOYONES EN CREMA DE FRIJOL

serves 8

FOR THE DUMPLINGS:

1 pound (455 g) fresh masa (see Notes, page 80)

Salt

½ cup (105 g) lard or vegetable shortening, melted and cooled slightly

FOR THE BEAN CREMA:

5 cups (975 g) cooked pinto beans, plus 3 cups (720 ml) cooking liquid (see page 18)

1 cup (240 ml) heavy cream

(ingredients continue on page 80)

TO MAKE THE DUMPLINGS:

❧ Place the masa in a large bowl and break it up with your fingers into small pieces. Add ¾ teaspoon salt, pour in the lard or shortening, and mix with a spoon until nearly incorporated. Use your hands to knead the dough to fully incorporate the ingredients, about 5 minutes.

❧ Scoop up portions of dough to form *chochoyones* (dumplings) about 1¼ inches (3 cm) in diameter. Lightly press the tip of your thumb into the center of the ball to make a small divot. Continue making *chochoyones* until all the masa has been used to make about 48 balls. Set them aside on a baking sheet as you make them and bring a large pot of water to a boil over high heat.

TO MAKE THE BEAN CREMA:

❧ In a large, wide saucepan, bring the beans with their boiling liquid to a soft boil over medium heat. Add the cream and blend with an immersion blender, adding water or more bean boiling liquid if needed to give it a soupy consistency. Season with salt and return to a simmer.

(recipe continues on page 80)

Finely grated Cotija cheese
(see Notes)

Crushed red pepper flakes

1 hoja santa leaf, cut into
chiffonade (optional; see
Notes)

TO COOK THE DUMPLINGS:

⚡ In batches, add the dumplings to the pot of boiling water. Like gnoc-chi, they will float to the surface when they are ready, 3 to 4 minutes. Scoop them out with a slotted spoon, drain off excess water, and place them on a baking sheet. When all of the dumplings are cooked, drop them into the bean *crema*. Bring to a simmer and cook for 5 minutes to meld the flavors.

TO PLATE:

⚡ Spoon a stack of dumplings into the center of a bowl and carefully pour in some bean *crema*. Garnish each bowl with some Cotija cheese, a pinch of crushed red pepper flakes, and a little hoja santa, if using.

notes

Using instant corn flour doesn't work with this recipe. I tried playing with the recipe to include it as an option, but both the flavor and tex-ture do not turn out right.

This recipe serves 8 generously, and there very well may be *recalenta-dos* (reheated leftovers) the following day. Don't worry; after the effort of making these delicious dumplings, you will thank me because no doubt you will want this dish again! If you have a small family like me, you can freeze your *chochoyones* before cooking them and save them for a rainy day.

If you can't find Cotija cheese, feel free to use another Mexican cheese or any type of melting or crumbling cheese.

Though the hoja santa is optional, if you can find this velvety, flavorful leaf, you should really consider using it. Often called pepper leaf or yerba santa, it is also known as the "root beer plant" owing to its aroma.

Rajas translates to "slices." So you can already imagine what this dish is going to look like. This recipe calls for fire-roasted poblano chiles, which are balanced out with the sweetness of yellow corn and the creaminess of queso fresco and a light cream sauce. It's a recipe that my vegetarian friends will thank me for! Serve with Mexican Red Rice (page 140) and Traditional Refried Beans (page 143).

poblano chile slices and queso fresco

RAJAS CON QUESO

serves 4 to 6

6 poblano peppers, roasted (see page 69)

1 tablespoon canola oil

½ yellow onion, diced

2 garlic cloves, sliced

2 medium Roma tomatoes, chopped

1½ cups (220 g) fresh corn kernels (from 2 ears corn)

¾ cup (180 ml) vegetable or chicken stock

½ cup (120 ml) heavy cream

Salt and freshly ground black pepper

1 pound (455 g) queso fresco, cut into ½-inch (12-mm) cubes

❧ Slice the roasted poblanos into ½-inch (12-mm) strips.

❧ Heat the oil in a large deep skillet over medium-high heat. Reduce the heat to medium, add the onion, and cook for 1 to 2 minutes, until transparent. Add the garlic and sauté for 1 minute, or until fragrant. Add the tomatoes and cook until they begin to break down, about 2 minutes. Add the corn and continue cooking for another 2 minutes, or until the corn starts to soften. Add the stock, cover, and bring to a simmer.

❧ Reduce the heat to medium-low and simmer until the corn is tender, 3 to 5 minutes. Add the cream and return it to a simmer. Season with salt and pepper, then add the poblanos and cheese. Mix carefully to combine the ingredients without breaking up the cheese too much. Cover and allow it to simmer for another 5 minutes to meld the flavors. Remove from the heat and allow the mixture to rest for 3 minutes before serving.

notes
To keep this dish vegetarian, use vegetable stock rather than chicken stock.

While growing in popularity in authentic Mexican restaurants in the United States, *huitlacoche* has yet to truly gain the respect it deserves. Known as the truffle of Mexican cooking (and also known as corn smut, a fungus that grows on corn), when cooked correctly and seasoned appropriately, this unseemly ingredient can truly be one of the most delicious delicacies around.

I served this as my finale appetizer as a way of both embracing the cuisine of Mexico and speaking to the beginning of my personal culinary story. Since tamales are one of the first recipes I learned to make, it was only right that I would begin such an important menu with a dish that represented both the humble ingredients I grew up cooking with and an ingredient that was more refined. These step-by-step photos will guide you in making these little pockets of amazingness.

huitlacoche tamales

TAMALES DE HUITLACOCHE

makes 20 to 24 tamales

FOR THE TAMALE MASA:

1 (6-ounce/170-g) package dried cornhusks

2 pounds (910 g) fresh corn masa or 6 cups (780 g) instant corn masa flour such as Maseca

1 tablespoon salt

1½ teaspoons baking powder

5 cups (1.2 L) vegetable or chicken stock (if using instant corn flour)

1 cup (205 g) lard or vegetable shortening, melted and cooled slightly

(ingredients continue)

TO MAKE THE TAMALES:

⚹ Bring a large pot of water to a boil. Remove from the heat and add the cornhusks. Place a weight on top of the cornhusks to hold them under water (a *molcajete*—mortar and pestle—works great for this). Soak for 10 to 30 minutes, until the husks are pliable. Transfer to a strainer to drain.

⚹ Place the fresh corn masa or instant corn flour in the bowl of a stand mixer fitted with the paddle attachment (if you're using fresh masa, break it up with your hands into small pieces). Add the salt and baking powder and mix on low speed to combine. If using instant corn flour, add the stock and mix until combined. For fresh or instant, stream in the melted lard or shortening and mix until combined, then increase the speed to medium-high and mix for an additional 5 to 10 minutes, until the mixture is light and fluffy. If you're using instant corn flour, cover and refrigerate for 20 minutes before proceeding.

(recipe continues)

TO MAKE THE FILLING:

⁑ Heat the oil in a large sauté pan over medium-high heat. Quickly add the onion, garlic, and chile and cook, stirring, for 2 minutes. Add the *huitlacoche* and cook for an additional 2 minutes. Add the stock and bring to a simmer. Reduce the heat to medium-low, cover the pan, and simmer for 3 to 5 minutes, until the *huitlacoche* is tender and can be pressed between two fingers (it will already be soft if you're using canned *huitlacoche*). Remove the lid and continue to simmer until the liquid is completely absorbed. Season with salt and pepper and remove from the heat to cool.

TO ASSEMBLE THE TAMALES:

⁑ Fill a tamale-steaming pot (see Notes, page 88) with about 2 inches (5 cm) of salted water.

⁑ Find the largest cornhusks with no holes or imperfections. Remove any stray corn hairs and lay the husks on your work surface with the smooth, waxy-side up, rough-side down, and the narrow end facing you. Place about ½ cup (120 ml) of the masa mixture (more or less depending on the size of the cornhusk) in the center of the cornhusk and spread it with the back of a spoon to an even layer just under ¼ inch (6 mm), filling the entire cornhusk from edge to edge, leaving about a 1½-inch (4-cm) space at the narrowest part of the corn husk where you are holding it (this area will be folded).

⁑ Pick up your cornhusk and cradle it in the cup of your nondominant hand, narrowest end facing you, allowing the extra cornhusk to drape over your pinky and thumb. Creating this pocket will allow you to work efficiently without losing any of your tamale filling. Add a heaping tablespoon of *huitlacoche* to the center of your cornhusk, topped by a piece of cheese and a sprinkle of cilantro. Do not overfill.

⁑ Fold one side of the husk over the filling, then fold the other side to seal your tamale. Then fold the narrow end of your tamale up toward the open side, sealing the bottom. You can either keep them folded or tie them together with a long strip of cornhusk—it's up to you.

⁑ As you make each tamale, set it in the steaming basket (see Notes, page 88) on its folded bottom. When all the tamales are in the steamer, place a layer or two of the remaining cornhusks on top to cover the

(recipe continues on page 88)

FOR THE FILLING:

2 tablespoons canola oil

⅓ cup (40 g) finely diced red onion

1 large garlic clove, minced

1 serrano chile, thinly sliced

1 pound (455 g) fresh *huitlacoche* (see Notes) or 3 (7-ounce/200-g) cans *huitlacoche*

1 cup (240 ml) vegetable or chicken stock

Salt and freshly ground black pepper

10 to 12 ounces (280 to 340 g) Oaxaca cheese or Monterey Jack cheese, pulled or cut into ½-ounce (15-g) rectangular strips

¼ cup (10 g) finely chopped fresh cilantro leaves

ACCOMPANIMENTS (OPTIONAL)

Oaxacan Avocado Cream (page 40)

Cactus Salsa (page 37)

Crispy Pork Chicharrón (page 146)

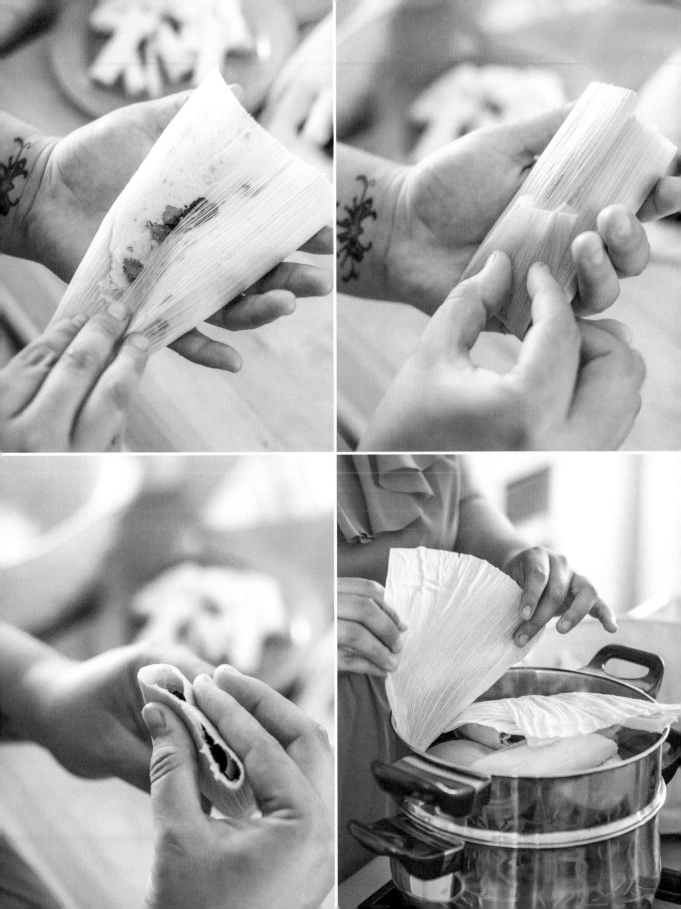

tamales completely. Cover the pot, set it over medium-low heat, and bring to a simmer. Steam the tamales for about 90 minutes, checking every 20 minutes to see if the pot needs more hot water. Remove a tamale; let it rest for 1 minute and check it. It's done when the cornhusk peels away from the tamale with ease. If not, give them a few more minutes and check again. Allow the tamales to rest for 5 minutes, then serve with any or all of the suggested accompaniments.

notes

Fresh *huitlacoche* can be difficult to find. If you are only able to locate the canned form, don't fret. With the added flavors of the onion, garlic, and serrano chile, your tamales will be just as delicious.

If you don't have a tamale steamer or steamer basket, use an upside-down metal strainer. It works just as well!

Have a pressure cooker? You can cut your steaming time by about half by using a pressure cooker to steam your tamales (all the steps for making the tamales are the same). That's how I was able to make this dish in the sixty minutes I had for the finale.

Up to this point in the season (Top 5), the men were bringing it in the creative department, winning every single "Mystery Box Challenge." Until I got to dreaming—literally—of what might be thrown my way.

I have always been spiritual, but the next "Mystery Box Challenge" was as if God handed me everything I wanted. Not only had I dreamt about tomatoes the night before, but I dreamt of a dish I could make that required only one ingredient (aside from the staple pantry box): a tomato. So I said a little prayer, trusted my gut, and boy, oh boy, did it pay off! I was the only woman to win a Mystery Box that season. *Si se puede!* (It can be done!)

savory tomato napoleon

NAPOLEON DE TOMATE A LA MEXICANA

serves 4

FOR THE TORTILLA LAYERS:

2 cups (250 g) all-purpose flour, plus extra for dusting

1 teaspoon salt, plus more for sprinkling

⅓ cup (75 ml) canola oil, plus more for frying

¾ cup (180 ml) warm water

(ingredients continue on page 92)

TO MAKE THE TORTILLAS:

≫ Whisk together the flour and salt in a large bowl. Add the oil and mix until it resembles the texture of cornmeal (use your hands to break up large clumps if needed). Slowly pour the warm water into the bowl, stirring with a wooden spoon to fully incorporate it.

≫ Turn the dough out onto a lightly floured work surface and knead it for 5 minutes. The dough may be sticky initially, but as you continue kneading and dusting your work surface, the dough will become soft and warm and will no longer stick to the surface. Shape the dough into a ball, wrap it in plastic wrap, and allow it to rest for 10 minutes.

≫ Meanwhile, heat about 3 inches (7.5 cm) of oil in a shallow high-sided skillet to 375°F (190°C). If you don't have a frying thermometer, toss a scrap of dough into the oil; when it sizzles, it's ready.

≫ Divide the dough into quarters. Place one quarter of the dough in your hands and roll it into a ball with your palms. Place it on a generously floured work surface and flatten it with your hands into a 5-inch (12-cm) disc. Using a floured rolling pin, roll the dough out into an oblong shape as thin as possible—to the thickness of a store-bought tortilla, which is about 1/16 inch (2 mm) thick. Using either a pastry cutter or a knife, cut each quarter into as many 2 x 4-inch (5 x 10-cm)

(recipe continues on page 92)

savory tomato napoleon
(page 89)

FOR THE TOMATO SAUCE:

3 large salad tomatoes

1 tablespoon olive oil

2 shallots, minced

3 garlic cloves, crushed then minced

1 cup (240 ml) chicken stock, plus more if needed

1 tablespoon dried Mexican oregano

8 fresh basil leaves, julienned

Salt and freshly ground black pepper

FOR THE CRISPY TOMATO SKINS:

Reserved tomato skins from the sauce

1 tablespoon olive oil

FOR THE ROASTED TOMATOES:

6 medium tomatoes, cut in half then quartered

6 garlic cloves, crushed

2 tablespoons balsamic vinegar

3 tablespoons olive oil

rectangles as possible, reserving the scraps of dough. Repeat with the remaining quarters until you have twelve rectangles. Cut the scraps into thin triangle-shaped strips and set aside.

» Working in batches, fry both the rectangles and the triangles in the oil for about 2 minutes, until puffed and golden brown, pressing on them with a slotted spoon to keep them submerged in the oil and turning them halfway through to evenly brown them. As each batch is fried, drain it on paper towels and immediately season with salt.

» Preheat the oven to 300°F (150°C).

TO MAKE THE TOMATO SAUCE:

» Bring a medium pot of water to a boil. Use a paring knife to slice "X" cuts into the bottom of each tomato. Lower the tomatoes into the boiling water and blanch for 30 seconds to 2 minutes (depending on how ripe the tomatoes are), until the skins start to come away from the flesh, then remove them with a slotted spoon and immediately place them into an ice bath. Remove the tomatoes from the ice bath, pat them dry with paper towels, and peel off the skins in the largest pieces possible. Reserve the skins and chop the tomatoes.

» In a medium saucepan, heat the oil over medium heat. Add the shallots and sauté until translucent, about 2 minutes. Add the garlic and sauté until lightly browned, about 2 minutes. Add the chopped tomatoes and sauté for an additional 2 to 4 minutes, until the tomatoes begin to break down. Add the stock and bring to a simmer. Add the oregano, reduce the heat to medium-low, and cook until the tomatoes have completely broken down and the sauce has thickened, 30 to 35 minutes. If any large pieces remain, break them down with the back of a spoon. Add the basil and season with salt and pepper.

MEANWHILE, MAKE THE TOMATO SKINS:

» Line a baking sheet with a silicone baking mat.

» Brush the reserved tomato skins with the oil and season with salt and pepper. Arrange them in a single layer on the silicone mat. Place them in the oven and roast for 10 to 15 minutes, checking on them every 3 to 5 minutes, until the skins are dried and crisp. (The skins can be made up to 1 hour ahead, as they will stay crisp.)

TO MAKE THE ROASTED TOMATOES:

✳ Increase the oven temperature to 425°F (220°C).

✳ In a large bowl, toss the tomatoes with the garlic, vinegar, and oil. Spread the tomatoes onto an ungreased baking sheet and season with salt and pepper. Place in the oven and roast for 15 to 20 minutes, until the skins begins to blister.

TO PLATE:

✳ Spoon 1 tablespoon of the tomato sauce onto the center of each of four plates and top with a tortilla strip (the sauce serves as an anchor). Top with some roasted tomatoes and garlic and spoon 1 tablespoon tomato sauce over the top. Repeat to make three layers on each plate, finishing each napoleon with more sauce and some of the tortilla triangles. Drizzle a little sauce around the plate (you'll have some sauce left over) and garnish with the crispy tomato skins. Congratulations! You just made my Mystery Box–winning dish!

notes

What makes these tortillas different from my family's basic Flour Tortillas (page 22) is that for this challenge I had to make a tortilla recipe using only staple pantry box ingredients, which meant I didn't have access to lard and swapped in canola oil. The result was a vegetarian tortilla variation that most people can make with what they already have in their pantries.

This recipe is dedicated to my brother and twin sisters, whom I love dearly (interesting fact: Of the four, I'm the only one who isn't gay). We don't always agree on everything, but we come together on recipes like this one, which is a favorite of theirs. I love how food connects us no matter what the distance. So when my sister Marlia calls me from Texas to tell me she is making these enchiladas, my heart warms, because what she is really saying is that she misses me.

Serve with beans and rice for a complete meal, or do what I do and serve yourself a plate of three enchiladas!

green chicken enchiladas

ENCHILADAS VERDES DE POLLO

serves 4 to 6

FOR THE ENCHILADA SAUCE:

1 pound (455 g) fresh tomatillos

2 fresh Anaheim chiles, stemmed, cut in half, and deveined

1 jalapeño chile, stemmed, cut in half, and deveined

½ yellow onion, chopped

4 small garlic cloves, peeled

Salt

FOR THE CHICKEN:

½ yellow onion, peeled

4 garlic cloves, peeled

¼ teaspoon black peppercorns

(ingredients continue)

TO MAKE THE ENCHILADA SAUCE:

✣ Peel the husks off the tomatillos and rinse them thoroughly under lukewarm water until their skin is smooth and they are no longer tacky or sticky.

✣ Place the tomatillos, Anaheim chiles, jalapeño, and onion in a medium saucepan and add enough hot water to cover. Place over medium-high heat, bring to a simmer, then reduce the heat to medium-low and simmer until the tomatillos change color and everything just starts to soften, about 5 minutes. Remove the ingredients from the pan using a slotted spoon (reserve the liquid) and place them in the blender along with the garlic. Add ¼ cup (60 ml) of the tomatillo cooking liquid and blend on medium-low speed to a runny sauce consistency. If it's too thick, add more of the tomatillo cooking liquid.

✣ Pour the sauce into a saucepan and season with salt. Set over low heat, bring to a simmer, and simmer for 15 minutes. Remove the sauce from the heat, cover, and set aside until you're ready to put together your enchiladas (reheat the sauce just before assembling if needed).

TO MAKE THE CHICKEN:

✣ While the enchilada sauce is simmering, fill a 4-quart (3.8-L) saucepan two-thirds full with hot water. Bring to a boil over high heat, then add the onion, garlic, peppercorns, and salt to the water. Cut the

(recipe continues)

2 tablespoons salt

4 bone-in chicken leg quarters (about 2½ pounds/1.2 kg)

Canola oil, for frying

12 (6-inch/15-cm) corn tortillas, homemade (see page 20) or store-bought

Sour cream

Crumbled Cotija cheese

Chopped fresh cilantro

chicken leg quarters in half at the joint to separate the leg and thigh meat and remove the skin and excess fat. Add them to the pan, cover, reduce the heat to low, and check after 10 minutes to remove any foam that may be floating on top, taking care not to remove any pepper-corns or garlic. Cook for another 10 minutes, or until the chicken is cooked through.

⤐ Remove the chicken from the cooking liquid using a slotted spoon or tongs and set it aside in a colander to drain and cool for 15 minutes. Using a pair of forks or your hands, shred the chicken into even bite-size pieces, discarding the bones.

TO FRY THE TORTILLAS:

⤐ Set a small skillet over medium heat and add oil to cover the bottom of the pan by about ¼ inch (6 mm). When the oil begins to smoke, carefully add one tortilla and cook it on each side for about 30 seconds, just until it puffs up. Remove it from the oil onto a paper towel–lined plate. Repeat with the remaining tortillas, adding more oil to the pan as needed.

TO BUILD YOUR ENCHILADAS:

⤐ Place a tortilla on a plate, add some shredded chicken meat to the half of the tortilla closest to you, and top it with about 1 tablespoon of the warm enchilada sauce. Roll the tortilla tightly away from you to form an enchilada and place it on a serving plate seam-side down. Repeat with a second enchilada and smother the enchiladas with addi-tional sauce. Repeat with the remaining tortillas, chicken, and sauce, putting two or three enchiladas on each plate. Garnish the enchiladas with sour cream, Cotija cheese, and cilantro.

notes

If you have leftover Tomatillo Salsa (page 35), you can use it to make these enchiladas instead of the tomatillo sauce here; you may need to dilute it with a bit of chicken stock or water for the right consistency and to tone down the heat.

The enchilada sauce and chicken can be prepped long before you make these—up to a couple of days in advance. This is the perfect way to put together components on a Sunday for a weekday meal that the whole family will love.

Whenever I think of summer grilling, this is the first recipe that comes to mind. The tangy, vibrant marinade makes the most common of proteins a delight to eat. This is by far one of my favorite recipes to make for large family parties, and I hope you are able to create as many memories with this recipe as I have.

One of my favorite memories is of my late Tio Cuate grilling chicken in his backyard. I can't remember why we were there—it must have been someone's birthday—but I remember my *tio* and mom were singing and dancing by the grill. This *tio*, my favorite uncle, was a vibrant man who always radiated good energy to those around him, something I try to replicate in my life. So I dedicate this special recipe to him.

I hope your summer barbecues are as fun, zesty, and vibrant as this recipe!

grilled cilantro-lime chicken

POLLO ASADO MARINADO CON LIMÓN Y CILANTRO

serves 4

8 bone-in chicken thighs (about 3 pounds/1.4 kg; see Notes, page 99)

Salt and freshly ground black pepper

½ cup (20 g) finely chopped fresh cilantro leaves

1 teaspoon lemon zest

½ teaspoon lime zest

1 small yellow onion, thinly sliced

(ingredients continue)

✣ Remove the skin from the chicken (see Notes, page 99) and place the chicken in a deep nonreactive dish or baking pan in one layer. Season it generously with salt and pepper on both sides. Sprinkle on the cilantro, lemon zest, and lime zest. Next, layer the onion slices on top as evenly as possible, then pour the lemon and lime juices over the chicken. Drizzle the oil over the chicken and cover the dish with plastic wrap.

✣ Refrigerate for 4 hours, turning the chicken after about 2 hours (see Notes).

✣ Set an outdoor grill to medium heat or preheat an indoor grill pan over medium heat. Toss the chicken in the marinade once more to make sure it is completely coated with the oil—this will not only help your chicken crisp up beautifully, but it will also prevent it from sticking

(recipe continues)

to your grill. Generously season with more salt and pepper to balance the tartness of the marinade.

✸ Remove the chicken from the marinade and place it on the grill with the onion slices and a few lime wedges if you like. Cook for 5 to 7 minutes on each side, until the internal temperature reaches 155°F (65°C). Remove it from the heat to a platter, cover with aluminum foil, and set aside for about 10 minutes, until the chicken reaches the target temperature of 165°F (75°C).

⅓ cup (75 ml) fresh lemon juice

⅓ cup (75 ml) fresh lime juice

¼ cup (60 ml) canola oil

Lime wedges (optional)

notes

This recipe calls for bone-in dark chicken meat. This is my personal preference and what I grew up with, as bone-in chicken tends to have more flavor and dark meat is more common in Mexican dishes. However, you can choose to use boneless chicken or breast meat, keeping in mind that you will need to adjust the timing to keep it from drying out. Use a lower heat level for a longer amount of time to make sure your chicken doesn't char too much on the outside and end up raw on the inside. We all know Chef Ramsay would call us on that!

I call for removing the skin from the chicken so that the delicious marinade can best penetrate the meat.

As with any meat, the longer you marinate it, the more depth of flavor you'll be rewarded with. However, because the marinade is highly acidic, you don't want to marinate it too long or it will overpower the chicken. If time is short, you can trim the marinating time to as little as 30 minutes, which will still produce super-flavorful results.

The first time I tried chicken cordon bleu, I was very young and remember thinking, "Well, that could've been better" (no disrespect to the French). You see, growing up Mexican means you favor vibrant and spicy flavors. And, sadly, a traditional cordon bleu just didn't pack that kind of punch. My Mexican version replaces Swiss cheese with Oaxaca cheese and ham with chorizo.

The consistency of Mexican chorizo varies depending on whether it's prepackaged or ground up at the butcher. Usually a freshly ground chorizo will be meaty and less oily. If you are working with packaged chorizo, you may need to either strain or cook it down a bit longer in order to gain the right consistency, which is like a thick ground beef.

mexican cordon bleu

CORDON BLEU A LA MEXICANA

serves 6

8 ounces (225 g) fresh ground or packaged soft chorizo

¼ teaspoon dried Mexican oregano, divided

6 (8-ounce/225-g) boneless skinless chicken breasts, butterflied

3 ounces (85 g) Oaxaca cheese or Monterey Jack cheese, pulled or cut into ½-ounce (15-g) strips or rectangles

Salt and freshly ground black pepper

Canola oil

Chipotle Cream Sauce (page 42), warmed

Sautéed Chayote and Red Cabbage (page 135)

» Preheat the oven to 350°F (175°C).

» Heat a small sauté pan over medium heat. Add the chorizo and ⅛ teaspoon of the oregano and cook, stirring every 20 to 30 seconds to ensure there is no sticking, for 8 to 10 minutes, until the fat is rendered, the color darkens, and the meat is cooked through. Pour off any excess oil, transfer the chorizo to a plate, and let it cool completely.

» Open the chicken and place one-sixth of the cooked chorizo inside each one, along with ½ ounce (15 g) of the cheese. Close the butterflied chicken completely and seal with toothpicks or bamboo skewers. Season the outside of the chicken on both sides with salt and pepper and the remaining oregano.

» Heat a large sauté pan over medium-high heat and add just enough oil to coat the bottom. Sear the chicken breasts on all sides, including the top, 1 to 2 minutes per side, until the chicken is nicely browned all over. You may need to cook the breasts in batches or use two pans if available.

✵ Place the seared chicken breasts on a baking sheet and place them in the oven to finish cooking, another 10 to 15 minutes, until the internal temperature reaches 160°F (70°C; the temperature will continue to rise a little as it rests).

✵ Remove the chicken from the oven and allow it to rest for 3 to 4 minutes.

✵ To plate, cut each chicken breast into three gorgeous slices (trimming the ends). Smother them with Chipotle Cream Sauce (page 42) and serve them with Sautéed Chayote and Red Cabbage (page 135).

I will never forget the look on Olivia's and Hetal's faces when they first saw the animal heads revealed as part of one of our Mystery Box Challenges. I can understand how difficult that must have been for them, coming from backgrounds that were so different from mine. I grew up on a ranch, where we focused on rustic cooking using every part of the animal with nothing going to waste. In a funny way, I was happy to see a pig's head under that box.

These tostadas can really be made with an equal weight of any non-lean cut of pork meat, but I assure you, if you have never had pork cheek, there is no time like the present!

braised pork cheek tostada stacks with chipotle sour cream and pineapple-mango salsa

TOSTADA DE CACHETE DE PUERCO CON CREMA AGRIA DE CHIPOTLE Y SALSA DE PIÑA Y MANGO

makes 4 tostada stacks

FOR THE BRAISED PORK CHEEKS:

6 pork cheeks (about 4 ounces/ 115 g each), trimmed

8 garlic cloves, peeled

1 yellow onion, cut in half

2 tablespoons dried Mexican oregano

2 tablespoons salt

12 (6-inch/15-cm) corn tortillas, homemade (see page 20) or store-bought

TO MAKE THE PORK CHEEKS:

» Combine the pork cheeks, garlic, onion, oregano, and salt in a pressure cooker. Pour in enough water to make the pork cheeks float, place the pot over high heat, and bring the liquid to a boil. Reduce the heat to medium, secure the lid according to the manufacturer's instructions, bring it to high pressure, and cook for 45 minutes.

TO MAKE THE CHIPOTLE SOUR CREAM:

» Combine the sour cream and chipotle in a blender or food processor and blend until smooth. Transfer the sour cream to a bowl and season with salt. Place it in squeeze bottle and refrigerate until ready to serve.

TO MAKE THE SALSA:

» In a medium bowl, toss together the pineapple, mango, jalapeño, onion, lemon and lime juices, and cilantro. Season with salt and pepper. Set aside in a cool spot.

TO FINISH THE PORK CHEEKS:

⊁ Remove the pot from the heat and release the pressure from the pressure cooker. Remove the meat from the braising liquid, reserving the liquid. Using two forks, finely shred the meat. Place the shredded meat in a medium saucepan and add just enough braising liquid to top off the meat. Keep it warm over low heat.

TO FRY THE TORTILLAS:

⊁ In a deep fryer or skillet, heat at least 4 inches (10 cm) of oil to 375°F (190°C).

⊁ Use a 3-inch (7.5-cm) ring cutter, cut out 12 corn tortilla discs. Drop the discs into the oil one at a time, making sure not to overcrowd the fryer, and fry until crisp. Remove from the oil using tongs and place them on a paper towel–lined baking sheet to drain. Immediately season with salt.

TO MAKE THE SLAW:

⊁ You must wait until just before you are ready to serve to prepare your slaw, as you don't want it to go soft. In a medium bowl, toss the cabbage with the lemon and lime juices and season with salt and pepper.

NOW GET READY TO STACK:

⊁ Begin by placing a bed of slaw at the bottom of each of four plates to anchor the tostada. Add a fried tortilla and top it with some meat. Squeeze on some chipotle sour cream, spoon on a bit of slaw, and top it off with some salsa. Add a second fried tortilla and repeat to make a second layer. Top with a final tostada, finish with some salsa, and garnish with cilantro sprigs or even a few Crispy Pigs' Ears (page 145) strips like I did on the show!

Canola oil, for frying

Cilantro sprigs

FOR THE CHIPOTLE SOUR CREAM:

¾ cup (180 ml) sour cream

1 chipotle chile in adobo sauce

Salt

FOR THE PINEAPPLE-MANGO SALSA:

1 cup (165 g) diced pineapple

1 cup (165 g) diced mango

1 jalapeño, minced

¼ cup (30 g) diced white onion

2 tablespoons fresh lemon juice

2 tablespoons fresh lime juice

¼ cup (10 g) chopped fresh cilantro

Salt and freshly ground black pepper

FOR THE RED CABBAGE SLAW:

2 cups (150 g) shredded red cabbage

1 tablespoon fresh lemon juice, or to taste

1 tablespoon fresh lime juice, or to taste

Salt and freshly ground black pepper

braised pork cheek tostada stacks with chipotle sour cream and pineapple-mango salsa (pages 102–103)

If you ask my mom what Munchkin's favorite food is, she will always tell you achiote pork chops. In fact, I can't make these delicious chops in my house without being reminded that this is my mom's recipe and that hers are the best. Munchkin cuts me no slack, no matter how good my version is!

Serve these chops with pineapple-mango salsa (see page 102) and shredded red cabbage as in the photo here. Or serving them up with Tabasco Green Beans (page 138) and some Oregano-Roasted Potatoes (page 139) would make for a mind-blowing meal, too!

achiote-rubbed pork chops

CHULETAS DE PUERCO EN ACHIOTE

serves 4

4 thick-cut boneless pork loin chops

Salt and freshly ground black pepper

2 tablespoons achiote paste

Juice of 1 orange (about ¼ cup/60 ml)

Pineapple-mango salsa (see page 102)

Shredded red cabbage (optional)

⊁ Preheat a grill pan over medium-high heat and preheat the oven to 400°F (205°C).

⊁ Season the pork chops generously with salt and pepper. Rub in the achiote paste well. (The more it is massaged into the meat, the more it penetrates it with color and flavor. Use gloves to avoid staining your fingers.)

⊁ Place the pork chops in a shallow nonreactive bowl. Pour the orange juice over the chops and set them aside to marinate for 5 to 10 minutes. (I know it doesn't seem like a long time, but the idea here is that you don't necessarily want the citrus to add a significant flavor but rather just a touch of citric undertones.)

⊁ Sear your chops on the grill pan for 1½ minutes on each side, then move the chops to an oven-safe skillet and bake for an additional 3 minutes, or until the internal temperature reaches 145°F (60°C). Remove from the oven and allow them to rest for 4 minutes before serving. Serve with pineapple-mango salsa and shredded red cabbage or any of your favorite sides.

As I have grown as a cook, I have always wanted to replicate my *mami's* signature dishes. Even now, it's still difficult to match her culinary prowess. Recently, though, I turned on the *banda* music in my kitchen and got to work, singing and dancing like my mom always does. I cooked with love, as I was taught to do.

When I was finished, I brought my pot full of chile verde to our ranch. I served my parents and our very close friends and paused for reaction. My dad immediately turned to me and told me, "*Hija esta carne de puerco te quedo igualita a la de tu mama* (Daughter, your pork dish came out the same as your mom's)!" They don't know it, but I turned around and shed two tears. It took me eight years to get it just right. *Ajuaaaa!* (Yippee!)

chile verde pork

CARNE DE PUERCO EN CHILE VERDE

serves 6

2½ pounds (1.2 kg) pork shoulder, cut into ¾-inch (2-cm) cubes

Salt and freshly ground black pepper

3 garlic cloves, sliced

1 medium yellow onion, chopped

2 cups (480 ml) Tomatillo Salsa (page 35)

Cilantro leaves (optional)

❧ Heat a large sauté pan over medium-high heat. Add the pork to the dry pan (the pork will render its own fat). Immediately season the pork with salt and pepper and cook for 5 minutes without moving it to render some of the fat; continue to cook until seared on all sides and there is no longer any pink showing, another 5 to 7 minutes.

❧ Add the garlic and onion and cook until the onion and garlic are fragrant and starting to soften, about 5 minutes. Stir in the salsa, bring it to a simmer, and reduce the heat to low. Check the seasoning and adjust with salt and pepper as needed. Cover and cook for 1¼ to 1½ hours, until the pork is fork-tender but not falling apart. Garnish with cilantro if you like and serve alongside Mexican Red Rice (page 140) and Traditional Refried Beans (page 143).

Mulitas are the ultimate taco-stand meal for me! Most people are there for tacos, but I love my *mulitas*—tacos with *queso* (cheese). This recipe is my version of the *mulitas* I grew up with, influenced by what I've picked up along the way from friends who have worked in various taco stands.

There is no right way to eat these delicious *mulitas*, but I recommend using the top tortilla to scoop up half of the contents and eating it like a taco, so in essence you have two yummy tacos with cheese. Oh, yes! *Provecho!*

pork adobada quesadillas

MULITAS DE CARNE ADOBADA

makes 8 quesadillas

6 dried guajillo chiles, stemmed and seeded

3 tablespoons achiote paste

4 garlic cloves, peeled

¼ cup (60 ml) pineapple juice from the canned pineapple (see page 112)

¼ cup (60 ml) fresh orange juice (from 1 medium orange)

¼ cup (60 ml) white vinegar

1 teaspoon crushed red pepper flakes

1 tablespoon dried Mexican oregano

1 tablespoon ground New Mexico chile powder

(ingredients continue)

↣ Place the guajillo chiles in a small saucepan. Add water to cover and place them over medium heat. Bring to a simmer and cook, pressing on them with tongs a few times to keep them submerged, until softened, about 5 minutes. Remove the chiles from the pan using a slotted spoon; place them in a blender along with the achiote paste, garlic, pineapple juice, orange juice, vinegar, crushed red pepper flakes, oregano, chile powder, and 2 teaspoons salt and blend into a thick adobada paste.

↣ Cut the pork into 1½ by 1-inch (4 by 2.5-cm) pieces, then thinly slice the pieces lengthwise. Place the pork in a large nonmetallic bowl and season it generously with salt and pepper. Add the adobada paste and mix until the meat is smothered in the paste. Cover the bowl with plastic wrap and refrigerate for a minimum of 2 hours or up to 24 hours (the longer you marinate the meat, the more flavorful it will be).

↣ Preheat a griddle or *comal* (tortilla griddle) over high heat to get it ready for the tortillas.

↣ Heat a separate, nonreactive large skillet over medium heat. Add the meat and pineapple, stir to combine, and cook for about 12 minutes, until the pork is fork-tender. Remove from the heat.

(recipe continues)

Salt

1½ pounds (680 g) pork rump roast

Freshly ground black pepper

1 (14.5-ounce/415-g) can no-sugar-added pineapple chunks, cut into ¼-inch (6-mm) pieces

16 (6-inch/15-cm) corn tortillas, homemade (see page 20) or store-bought

8 ounces (225 g) Oaxaca cheese or Monterey Jack cheese, thinly sliced

Oaxacan Avocado Cream (page 40)

½ cup (20 g) chopped fresh cilantro

½ cup (60 g) chopped yellow onion

Rustic Mexican Salsa (page 30) or Tomatillo Salsa (page 35)

✣ Reduce the heat to low and heat two tortillas on the griddle for about 30 seconds on each side, until malleable. Add about 1 ounce (28 g) of the cheese to one tortilla and flip it so the cheese is facing down. When the cheese has melted, use a fish spatula or another very thin spatula to flip over the tortilla and top it with a second tortilla. Immediately flip it over and continue to cook until the tortillas are fully cooked (but not crunchy) and the cheese is completely melted and on the verge of oozing out. Remove the quesadilla to a plate, separate the two tortillas, and slip in about ½ cup (120 ml) of cooked meat, a little avocado cream, about 1 tablespoon each of cilantro and onion, and a nice spoonful of salsa. Repeat with the remaining ingredients to make 8 quesadillas.

Sincronizadas, or "synchronized quesadillas," are pretty much just quesadillas made with two whole flour tortillas, with cheese (and usually ham) sandwiched between them. This no-folding quesadilla is easy to make and easy to assemble; it's perfect for a midafternoon or late evening snack. My fondest memories of these treats are when my brother, Josue, and I were allowed to stay up well past ten when the heat of the San Diego summer was in full swing.

This recipe says you can substitute corn tortillas for flour tortillas, and that's because you should use what you have. As a single mom, I often have to do that. So use whatever tortillas you have handy and synchronize them into some deliciousness!

synchronized quesadillas

QUESADILLAS SINCRONIZADAS

makes 6 quesadillas

12 flour or corn tortillas, homemade (see page 22 or 20) or store-bought

Canola oil or cooking spray

6 slices ham

12 ounces (340 g) Oaxaca cheese or Monterey Jack cheese, pulled or cut into strips

¼ cup (60 ml) Chipotle Cream Sauce (page 42)

Traditional Guacamole (page 129)

Sour cream

❧ Heat a griddle or *comal* (tortilla griddle) over medium heat.

❧ Unless freshly made, heat the tortillas on each side for 30 seconds, or until pliable, placing them in a tortilla warmer or wrapping them in a clean kitchen towel as you make them.

❧ Add a small drizzle of oil to the griddle and brush it over the entire surface (or coat the pan with cooking spray). Place one slice of ham on the griddle and cook for 30 seconds on each side. Add 2 ounces (55 g) of cheese to the top of the ham slice and cook for another 30 seconds, or until it's just starting to melt.

❧ Using a basting brush, generously brush a tortilla with Chipotle Cream Sauce on one side. Flip the tortilla on top of the cheese and ham slice, then use a spatula to flip the whole thing over so you have an open-faced quesadilla. Place a second tortilla on top of the cheese and ham and press down with spatula. Continue cooking for 1 to 2 minutes on each side, until the cheese starts to ooze out of the sides. Repeat to make 6 synchronized quesadillas.

❧ Slice the quesadillas into 6 triangles by cutting the circle three times like a pizza. Serve them with guacamole and sour cream.

Birria is a slow-cooked protein stew flavored with a variety of chiles and spices. It's typically made from goat's or sheep's meat, though in the United States you will find that most *birria* recipes will call for beef, as goat and sheep are less commonly available. If you do have the opportunity to make yours with goat or sheep, prepare yourself for the best *birria* you have ever had!

This is a recipe we often make for large parties, as it can easily be doubled or quadrupled.

traditional spicy stewed meat

BIRRIA TRADICIONAL

serves 6

6 dried California chiles, stemmed and seeded

2 dried pasilla chiles, stemmed and seeded

2 dried guajillo chiles, stemmed and seeded

2 yellow onions, chopped, divided

6 garlic cloves, peeled

1½ tablespoons dried oregano

1 teaspoon ground cumin

3 pounds (1.4 kg) beef chuck roast or goat's or sheep's leg meat, cut into 6 to 8 equal pieces

10 black peppercorns

≫ Place the dried California, pasilla, and guajillo chiles in a medium saucepan and add water to cover. Place the pan over high heat and bring it to a boil. Turn off the heat, cover, and allow the chiles to rest for 5 to 10 minutes. Using tongs, remove the chiles from the saucepan and place them in a blender with about 2 cups (480 ml) of the boiling liquid, half of the chopped onion, the garlic, oregano, and cumin. Blend until smooth but not too thick, adding more of the reserved boiling liquid if needed.

≫ Place the meat in a large saucepan or Dutch oven and add water to just barely cover the meat. Add the peppercorns, bay leaves, and 1 tablespoon salt. Add the chile paste and stir to mix it in. Cover the pan, place it over medium heat, and bring to a boil. Reduce the heat to very low to maintain a bare simmer and cook for about 2 hours (don't worry about overcooking it—the longer you cook it, the better the flavor develops), until the meat is fork-tender and falling apart, gently mixing it every 30 minutes and checking the sauce level. The meat should be completely covered with braising liquid (see Notes); if not, add hot water and make sure the heat is not too high.

⇴ Remove one of the pieces of meat. Using tongs and a fork, break up the meat in the center of a shallow bowl and fill it with broth to cover the meat by three quarters. Repeat with the remaining meat and broth. Sprinkle on some cilantro and the remaining onion, garnish with a dried chile de árbol (crumble the chile to add more heat), and serve.

notes
Keeping the meat covered with braising liquid is important so that the meat cooks evenly and breaks apart perfectly for the final presentation.

4 medium bay leaves

Salt

Leaves from 1 small bunch cilantro, minced

6 dried chiles de árbol, fried or toasted

traditional spicy stewed
meat (page 114)

Carne asada is to Mexico what burgers are to the United States. We love it and eat it at least several times a month. I love this recipe because, like so many Mexican dishes, it elevates the simplest of ingredients to provide an explosion of flavor.

You can use any thin cut of beef, such as flank, skirt, or flap steak. If these aren't available, using any cut from the bottom part of a sirloin and having it sliced about ¼ inch (6 mm) thick will work. Trust me when I say that this is a cut above the rest (pun intended)!

traditional grilled skirt steak

CARNE ASADA TRADICIONAL

serves 4 to 6

2½ pounds (1.2 kg) skirt steak

2 tablespoons salt

2 tablespoons freshly ground black pepper

2 oranges, sliced into half moons

1 yellow onion, thinly sliced

Juice of 4 oranges (about 1 cup/240 ml)

⊁ Season the meat on both sides with the salt and pepper. Set a layer of meat in a large nonreactive container and cover it with some of the orange slices and onion slices. Cover that layer with more meat and repeat the layering until all the meat and orange and onion slices have been used.

⊁ Pour the orange juice over the meat, cover with plastic wrap, and refrigerate for 1 to 4 hours. The longer you marinate the meat, the more the citrus will penetrate and tenderize it.

⊁ Preheat a grill or grill pan to medium-high heat. Remove the steak from the marinade and discard the orange and onion slices. Grill the meat for 3 to 4 minutes on each side, until done to your liking. Do not flip it more than once. Depending on the thickness of your steak, you may need to cook it a bit longer on indirect heat to achieve the desired temperature of the steak. Serve it as whole steaks or chop them up to make carne asada tacos or tostadas.

You can get fish tacos at most places in Southern California. However, I know that they aren't as common across the rest of the United States and abroad, so I decided to share a little bit of Baja California with you through this recipe for Ensenada-style fish tacos.

What makes these tacos Ensenada-style is their unique sour cream sauce, a tangy mix of mayo and sour cream that they make in this port town on the Pacific Ocean. Crack open a beer, squeeze on some fresh lime, and get transported to your own Baja vacation.

ensenada-style fish tacos

TACOS DE PESCADO ESTILO ENSENADA

makes 16 tacos

Canola oil, for frying

FOR THE ENSENADA-STYLE SOUR CREAM:

½ cup (120 ml) sour cream

⅓ cup (75 ml) mayonnaise

2 tablespoons fresh lime juice

1 tablespoon cold water

Salt and freshly ground black pepper

FOR THE DRY DREDGE:

⅔ cup (80 g) all-purpose flour

1 teaspoon salt

(ingredients continue)

❧ Fill a deep fryer with canola oil and heat it to 375°F (190°C).

TO MAKE THE SOUR CREAM:

❧ In a medium bowl, whisk together the sour cream, mayonnaise, lime juice, and water until completely incorporated and a little runny but not watery. If it's too runny, add little more sour cream and mayonnaise. Season with salt and pepper. Refrigerate until ready to use.

TO MAKE THE DRY DREDGE:

❧ In a shallow bowl, whisk together the flour, salt, pepper, and granulated garlic to incorporate.

TO MAKE THE FISH BATTER:

❧ In large shallow bowl, whisk together the flour, salt, pepper, paprika, and granulated garlic. Whisk in the eggs and beer. The mixture should be the consistency of pancake batter. If it is too thick, add a little more beer to thin it out.

(recipe continues)

1 teaspoon freshly ground black pepper

1 teaspoon granulated garlic

FOR THE FISH BATTER:

2 cups (250 g) all-purpose flour

1½ teaspoons salt

¼ teaspoon freshly ground black pepper

¼ teaspoon paprika

1 teaspoon granulated garlic

2 large eggs

2½ cups (600 ml) cold Mexican beer, plus more if needed

FOR THE TACOS:

2 pounds (910 g) skinless red snapper fillets

16 (6-inch/15-cm) corn tortillas, homemade (see page 20) or store-bought

2 cups (190 g) shredded red cabbage

Lime wedges (optional)

TO FRY THE FISH:

⊁ Set a cooling rack over a baking sheet to drain any residual fat (if you don't have a cooling rack, paper towels set over a flat plate will work too).

⊁ One at a time, add the red snapper fillets to the dry dredge and toss to coat. Transfer them to a plate or baking sheet. Working in batches, dredge the fish in the wet batter, letting any excess drip off, and carefully place them in the deep fryer. Fry for 3 to 5 minutes, until golden brown on both sides, flipping them once the underside is browned. Remove them to the wire rack to drain and immediately sprinkle with salt.

TO HEAT THE TORTILLAS:

⊁ While the fish is frying, preheat a skillet or *comal* (tortilla griddle) over high heat to get it nice and hot. Reduce the heat to low and warm the tortillas for about 1 minute on each side, until malleable, placing them in a kitchen towel as they are heated to keep them warm.

TO SERVE:

⊁ Place a piece of fried fish on each tortilla, top with shredded cabbage and Ensenada-style sour cream, and serve with lime wedges alongside if you like.

Developing a *MasterChef* finale entrée is like being asked what you'd like your last meal on earth to be. There was so much pressure riding on this one single dish—it had to be impressive, but, more importantly, it had to be *me* on a plate. I wanted to follow my appetizer (the Huitlacoche Tamales, page 82) with something that represented my heritage and family and also continued to tell my story. And when I thought back to the beginning of my story, it led me to my first visit to Mazatlán, watching the fishing boats coming into the port with their swordfish proudly hoisted up high and experiencing the exciting flavors, textures, and techniques of the region's cooking. This recipe is a trip through Mazatlán, both in flavor and in heart.

To make the dish exactly as I made it for the finale, serve it with Chorizo, Chayote, and Chickpea Sauté (page 133), Chickpea Fritters (page 136), and Tomatillo Salsa (page 35).

grilled swordfish with mexican squash and blistered tomatoes

PEZ ESPADA ASADO CON CALABACITA CURTIDA Y TOMATES SALTEADOS

serves 4

FOR THE GRILLED SWORDFISH:

4 (6-ounce/170-g) swordfish steaks (about 1 inch/2.5 cm thick)

Olive oil

3 tablespoons Goya Sazón (seasoning) without annatto

Salt

TO MAKE THE SWORDFISH:

⇗ Heat a grill pan over high heat.

⇗ Liberally brush the swordfish steaks with oil and dust with the Sazón (seasoning) and salt. Allow them to rest while you prepare the blistered tomatoes.

⇗ Place the swordfish on the grill pan and cook it for 2 minutes, give it a quarter turn to create crosshatch sear marks, and grill for an additional 2 minutes. Flip the steaks over and repeat on the other side, until the fish is just opaque, 2 to 4 minutes more. Remove the steaks from the pan and set them aside to rest for 5 minutes before serving.

TO MAKE THE BLISTERED TOMATOES:

✣ In a medium bowl, combine the cherry tomatoes, oil, and sugar and toss to combine. Heat a large skillet over high heat, add the tomatoes skin side down, and cook until they are blistered, 3 to 5 minutes. Season with a pinch of salt. Set aside.

TO MAKE THE SQUASH:

✣ Trim the top and bottom of the squash, and using a "Y" vegetable peeler or a mandoline, cut the squash into very thin ribbons from all sides, ending at the seeds in the middle. Discard the seeds. Place the squash in a bowl and toss it with the lime juice and oil. Season with salt. Just before plating, toss in a bit of the micro cilantro and some nasturtium leaves, if using.

TO PLATE:

✣ Smear a large tablespoon of the tomatillo salsa across a plate, if using. Add 2 heaping tablespoons of the chorizo, chayote, and chickpea sauté, if using, to the center of the plate. Place a grilled swordfish fillet on top and top it with the squash ribbons and their citrus vinaigrette. Serve with the blistered tomatoes and chickpea fritters on the side, if you like. Garnish with nasturtium leaves, if available.

FOR THE BLISTERED TOMATOES:

1 cup (145 g) cherry tomatoes, heirloom if available, halved

1 tablespoon olive oil

1 teaspoon sugar

Salt

FOR THE SQUASH:

1 (8-ounce/225-g) summer squash, preferably Mexican tatuma squash

2 tablespoons fresh lime juice

1 tablespoon olive oil

Salt

Micro cilantro and nasturtium leaves (optional)

FOR THE GARNISHES:

Tomatillo Salsa (page 35; optional)

Chorizo, Chayote, and Chickpea Sauté (page 133; optional)

Chickpea Fritters (page 136; optional)

*grilled swordfish
with mexican squash
and blistered tomatoes
(page 122)*

chickpea fritters
(page 136)

chorizo, chayote,
and chickpea sauté
(page 133)

sides

PARA ACOMPAÑAR

Before coming to the *MasterChef* kitchen, I really had to sit down and think about which side dishes I was going to develop to replace the Mexican staples of rice and beans. Americans are accustomed to the rice and beans served at the typical taco shop or stand. However, as I came to the *MasterChef* kitchen to prove, Mexican food is so much more than what you get at a Mexican fast food restaurant. There are many vibrant ingredients that can offer healthy, delicious alternatives to the tried-and-true rice and beans that will change your perception of what Mexican cooking can be. And in this chapter I will share several of them with you.

Every year for Cinco de Mayo, my friends would ask me for my traditional guacamole recipe. However, as with most home cooks, many of our family recipes are not written out with actual measurements. So I am happy to have a reason to finally write it all down and share this recipe with everyone.

Guacamole can be used in tacos and burritos, served with quesadillas, or just placed alongside a Rustic Mexican Salsa (page 30) and tortilla chips. No matter what your preference, make sure you include it on your grilled burgers—they will never be the same again.

traditional guacamole

GUACAMOLE TRADICIONAL

makes about 3 cups (720 ml)

4 medium ripe Hass avocados

½ cup (90 g) chopped tomato

¼ cup (30 g) minced onion

1 tablespoon minced jalapeño chile (see Notes)

¼ cup (10 g) chopped fresh cilantro leaves

½ teaspoon salt, or to taste

¼ teaspoon freshly ground black pepper, or to taste

1½ tablespoons fresh lime juice, or to taste (see Notes)

✳ Slice the avocados lengthwise around the pit and carefully remove the pit. Using a large spoon, scoop out the avocado flesh and place it in a large bowl. Using the back of a fork, mash the avocado until slightly smooth but still chunky. Mix in the tomato, onion, jalapeño, and cilantro. Add the salt and pepper, followed by the lime juice. Taste and adjust the seasonings. Serve immediately.

notes

You can seed and devein the jalapeño to reduce the heat level or omit it completely for people with milder tastes.

The lime juice prevents the guacamole from getting dark quickly. If you are preparing the guacamole in advance, squeeze the lime juice over the guacamole and then mix it in just before serving to keep it from turning dark. Covering your guacamole with plastic wrap will also help to keep its glorious green color.

I paired this frisée salad with my octopus dish (see page 57) in the *MasterChef* "Top 3" battle. Though salads are not a big part of Mexican cuisine, I knew that my octopus needed something acidic to balance it out, and the idea for this dish struck me immediately.

I chose to go with frisée because it's a bit more delicate and feminine than standard lettuce, yet holds its own in the flavor department. I added poblanos to give the salad a fire-roasted flavor and bring in a bit of heat. The vibrant honey-citrus-jalapeño vinaigrette adds a bright punch of flavor that cuts through the fire-roasted smokiness and brings all the flavors in the dish together.

frisée and poblano salad with honey-citrus-jalapeño dressing

ENSALADA DE FRISÉE Y POBLANO CON ADEREZO DE CITRICOS CON MIEL Y JALAPEÑO

serves 4

FOR THE DRESSING:

2 tablespoons fresh red grapefruit juice

1 tablespoon fresh lime juice

1 tablespoon fresh orange juice

2 tablespoons red wine vinegar

1½ tablespoons honey

¼ cup (60 ml) olive oil

1 teaspoon minced shallot

1 to 2 teaspoons minced jalapeño chile

Salt

FOR THE SALAD:

2 bunches frisée, separated into bite-size pieces (about 4 cups/160 g)

½ medium red onion, sliced into half moons

2 medium poblano chiles, roasted (see page 69) and sliced widthwise ¼ inch (6 mm) thick

TO MAKE THE DRESSING:

❧ In a medium bowl, whisk together the citrus juices, vinegar, and honey until the honey dissolves, then whisk in the oil. Stir in the shallot and jalapeño and season with salt.

TO MAKE THE SALAD:

❧ In a large bowl, toss the frisée with the red onion and poblanos. Whisk the salad dressing one more time, then immediately add some dressing to the vegetables and taste; continue to dress the salad until it's coated to your liking, taking care not to overdress it (you'll likely have extra dressing), and serve.

Now that you are a pro at getting *nopales* prepped (see page 17—or you cheated like I sometimes do and bought yourself a prepared bag), you are ready to make this amazing salad!

This dish was the one that convinced me I needed to give cactus another chance. Growing up, I wasn't a picky eater, but the slimy look of cactus always turned me off. Years later, I decided to give cactus another try at my goddaughter Cassandra's *quinceañera* and came up with this salad, which was served as a side to some amazing *carne asada* that we feasted on that memorable day.

cactus and queso fresco salad

NOPALES CON QUESO FRESCO

serves 6

Salt

1 pound (455 g) cactus paddles, cleaned (see page 16) and cut into ½-inch (12-mm) cubes

2 large Roma tomatoes, cubed

¼ cup (30 g) diced red onion

½ cup (20 g) chopped fresh cilantro leaves

½ teaspoon freshly ground black pepper

1 pound (455 g) queso fresco, cubed

» Bring a large saucepan of water to boil and season it well with salt. Add the cactus, return it to a boil, then reduce the heat and simmer for 3 to 4 minutes, until the pieces darken to a slightly muted green and are cooked through. Drain and let them cool.

» In a large bowl, combine the cactus, tomatoes, onion, cilantro, 1½ teaspoons salt, and the pepper. Gently fold in the queso fresco. Cover the bowl with plastic wrap and refrigerate for 1 hour before serving.

In developing this recipe, I wanted something to blow the flavor palates of the judges out of the water. I wanted to create a dish that I had never seen done, something that would deliver on both texture and flavor, and something that would show my evolution as a cook during my *MasterChef* journey.

This dish calls for fresh chickpeas, but I know that won't be an option in many regions. Don't fret—canned chickpeas are a great substitute—but if you can get your hands on some fresh chickpeas and don't mind peeling them out of their husks, that extra bite of texture will have you dancing around your kitchen!

chorizo, chayote, and chickpea sauté

CHAYOTE Y GARBANZO SALTEADO CON CHORIZO

serves 6

1 semi-firm chayote

8 ounces (225 g) fresh ground or packaged soft chorizo

1 tablespoon canola oil

½ medium yellow onion, minced

2 garlic cloves, minced

Salt and freshly ground black pepper

1 cup (185 g) husked fresh chickpeas (or substitute drained canned chickpeas)

⊁ Wash the chayote carefully with soap and water until the skin is no longer tacky. Slice the chayote in half lengthwise and, using a spoon or melon baller, remove the pit. Cut the chayote into thin julienne strips (use a mandoline if you have one).

⊁ Place a large sauté pan over medium heat. Add the chorizo and cook, stirring every 20 to 30 seconds to ensure there is no sticking, for 8 to 10 minutes, until the fat is rendered, the color darkens, and the meat is cooked through. Pour off any excess oil and allow the chorizo to rest.

⊁ Meanwhile, in separate sauté pan, heat the oil over medium heat. Add the onion and sauté for 30 seconds, then add the garlic and chayote and season with salt and pepper. Sauté for 3 to 4 minutes, stirring often, until the chayote starts to soften. Add the chickpeas and continue to cook until the chayote is tender and the chickpeas are warmed through, about 5 minutes.

⊁ Reduce the heat to low. Add the chorizo to the pan and stir until incorporated and warmed through, taking care not to break up the chayote, then serve.

Being of Mexican descent means I naturally lean toward colorful dishes with bright flavors; this dish is a perfect example.

Chayote squash, a staple vegetable in Mexican cuisine, is a key player in this recipe, with the slices of white and green squash providing contrast in texture and flavor to the vibrant purple-red cabbage.

This side is the perfect accompaniment to a *cena especial* (special dinner); I especially like to serve it alongside chicken dishes. You'll love it drizzled with Chipotle Cream Sauce (page 42).

sautéed chayote and red cabbage

CHAYOTE Y REPOLLO MORADO SALTEADO

serves 4 to 6

1 ripe chayote

1 tablespoon canola oil

2 garlic cloves, thinly sliced

¼ teaspoon crushed red pepper flakes

½ medium head red cabbage, cored and thinly sliced

½ teaspoon salt

¼ teaspoon freshly ground black pepper

❧ Wash the chayote carefully with soap and water until the skin is no longer tacky. Slice the chayote in half lengthwise and, using a spoon or melon baller, remove the pit. Place the chayote cut-side down onto a cutting board and slice it ⅛ inch (3 mm) thick.

❧ Heat the oil in a large sauté pan over medium-high heat. Add the garlic and sauté until it is fragrant, 30 to 60 seconds. Add the red pepper flakes and chayote and sauté until the chayote is just starting to soften, about 2 minutes. Add the red cabbage, salt, and pepper and sauté for an additional 2 to 3 minutes, until the chayote is fork-tender but the cabbage is still slightly crunchy. Serve.

notes

You are welcome to cook your cabbage all the way down, but keeping the cabbage a bit crunchy gives the dish a more complex texture and a vibrant flavor.

Garbanzos (chickpeas) are one of my mom's favorite ingredients. She loves to drop them into unorthodox dishes, which changes not only the flavor profile of those dishes but the texture as well. My mom's adventurous home-cook spirit has inspired me to push my own culinary boundaries.

This recipe was something I developed in the *MasterChef* kitchen during the finale to serve with my swordfish entrée (see page 122), and it has since made it onto my list of go-to dishes. I had never seen something like this done in Mexican cooking, but without innovation, we would never discover new and delicious flavor combinations. Not to mention the fact that Munchkin *loves* these—and I bet you will too!

chickpea fritters

BOLITAS DE GARBANZO

makes fourteen to sixteen 1½-inch (4-cm) fritters

1 tablespoon canola oil, plus more for frying

3 tablespoons minced yellow onion

1 garlic clove, minced

1 (15-ounce/430-g) can chickpeas, with liquid

1 teaspoon dried Mexican oregano

Salt and freshly ground black pepper

¾ cup (90 g) Wondra (instant) flour

⅔ cup (65 g) packaged crispy salted chickpeas

⁂ Heat the oil in a medium saucepan over medium-high heat. Add the onion and garlic and cook, stirring, for about 1 minute, until they are starting to soften. Add the chickpeas and their liquid and bring them to a simmer, stirring often. Add the oregano and season well with salt and pepper. Reduce the heat to low and mash the chickpeas with a potato masher until fairly smooth. Taste and adjust the seasoning as needed. Mix in ½ cup (60 g) of the flour.

⁂ Cover half of a baking sheet with plastic wrap and place the mashed chickpeas over it; spread them 1 inch (2.5 cm) thick with a spatula. Let them cool slightly, then place the baking sheet in the freezer for 8 to 12 minutes, until the chickpea mash is completely cooled but not frozen. (Or, if you have more time, let it cool completely and refrigerate until you're ready to fry.)

⁂ Meanwhile, in a spice grinder (working in two batches if needed), grind down the crispy chickpeas to a coarse sea-salt consistency. Place them in a bowl, add the remaining ¼ cup (30 g) flour, ¼ teaspoon salt, and some pepper, and toss with a fork to combine. Spread the mixture in a shallow dish.

꙳ Line a large plate with paper towels and set it close by. Remove the cooled chickpeas from the freezer and, using a 1½-inch (4-cm) scoop, form the mixture into balls and drop them into the crispy chickpea and flour mixture. Roll them around until generously covered and place the coated chickpea balls on a large plate.

꙳ Heat 3 inches (7.5 cm) of oil in a deep fryer or skillet over medium-high heat to 375°F (190°C). Drop in a few chickpea balls and fry them for 3 to 5 minutes, until browned all over. Remove them from the oil using a slotted spoon and place them on the paper towel–lined plate. Immediately sprinkle them with salt, let them cool for a couple of minutes, and serve.

Ejotes (green beans) were not a vegetable I was a fan of when I was a kid. However, I have a creative mom, and she mixed my green beans into scrambled eggs, along with other flavor boosters like garlic and onion, to make sure I would eat them. I came up with this dish to do the same for my Munchkin. Although most American children aren't used to eating Tabasco, my kid, like many Mexican children her age, is just starting to delve into the land of spicy food.

tabasco green beans
EJOTES AL TABASCO

serves 4

1 tablespoon canola oil

12 ounces (340 g) fresh green beans, trimmed

½ medium yellow onion, thinly sliced

4 garlic cloves, crushed and peeled

½ teaspoon salt

2 tablespoons Tabasco sauce

1 teaspoon Maggi sauce

» Before you start, open the windows or turn on the oven vent, as the fumes from the Tabasco can be quite strong.

» Heat a large sauté pan over medium-high heat until very hot. Quickly add the oil and green beans and sauté for 5 to 7 minutes, until they start to blister. Reduce the heat to medium, add the onion and garlic, and sauté for an additional 3 minutes, or until the onion is soft and transparent. Add the salt.

» Reduce the heat to low (reducing the heat is important in order to keep the Tabasco fumes under control), add the Tabasco and Maggi sauces, and cook for 1 to 2 minutes, tossing often to coat the beans, and serve.

notes

You can substitute any bottled hot sauce for the Tabasco, though the key here is not only heat but acidity, which vinegar-based Tabasco amply provides. If you're looking for acidity without heat, try substituting a lesser amount of red wine vinegar for the Tabasco.

One of my goals in developing recipes for the *MasterChef* competition was to revamp the techniques of tried-and-true recipes and dishes from other cultures by making use of Mexican spices and flavors. One of these recipe staples is rosemary-roasted potatoes. Though rosemary is a part of the Mexican pantry, it is not as commonly used as fragrant and flavorful oregano, and it's the oregano that really makes these potatoes stand out. I featured this dish in my "Top 3 Team Challenge" alongside my Grilled Achiote Octopus (page 57), but these potatoes are the perfect companion to any protein, as they will stand on their own even against the most vibrant of flavors.

oregano-roasted potatoes

PAPAS EN OREGANO

serves 4

1½ pounds (680 g) fingerling potatoes, cut in half lengthwise

2 tablespoons canola oil

½ teaspoon salt

¼ teaspoon freshly ground black pepper

¾ teaspoon dried Mexican oregano

⊰ Preheat the oven to 425°F (220°C).

⊰ Place the potatoes in large bowl, drizzle the oil over them, and toss with your hands to coat them in the oil.

⊰ Place the potatoes on a baking sheet in a single layer with a little space between each; make sure they don't overlap. Sprinkle the potatoes with the salt and pepper. Place the oregano in the cup of your palm and rub your hands together to break it while sprinkling it all over the potatoes.

⊰ Roast the potatoes for 25 to 35 minutes, until fork-tender inside and crisp on the outside, shaking the pan about 5 minutes in to make sure the potatoes don't stick to the pan. Remove the baking sheet from the oven and use a flat spatula to transfer the potatoes to a serving dish or plate.

Growing up, Mexican rice was as common as *frijoles* (beans), and in my family, rice is a part of almost every dinner meal. Note that this isn't what is commonly referred to as "Spanish" rice; this is Mexican red rice.

My Mexican red rice recipe calls for a spice called *azafrán bolita*. Originating from the state of Guanajuato, this spice is the Mexican version of saffron (though not actually related to saffron). It is a ball that is covered with a dark husk; when cracked open, it contains a bright yellow seed, which adds a saffron-colored hue to dishes it's cooked in. However, it can be hard to find (ask for it in Mexican groceries).

mexican red rice

ARROZ ROJO MEXICANO

serves 4

1 tablespoon canola oil

1 cup (185 g) long-grain white rice

¼ small onion, minced

1 garlic clove, minced

4 to 6 *azafrán bolita* pods (optional)

2 medium Roma tomatoes, chopped (see Notes)

1⅔ cups (405 ml) chicken stock (see Notes) or vegetable stock

1 teaspoon salt

↦ Heat the oil in a medium saucepan over medium heat. Add the rice and cook, stirring, until it is lightly colored all over, about 3 minutes. Add the onion and garlic and cook, stirring, for 1 minute, or until the onion is translucent.

↦ Meanwhile, use a mortar and pestle (or a *molcajete*, if you have one) to crack open the *azafrán bolita*, if using, and remove and discard the dark husks. Crush the yellow seeds in the mortar until they're pastelike and mix in 2 tablespoons of water to dilute it.

↦ Add the *azafrán bolita* liquid and the tomatoes to the rice and cook, stirring, for an additional 2 minutes, or until the tomato begins to cook down and release its red pigment into the rice.

↦ Pour in the stock, add the salt, and bring to simmer. Reduce the heat to low, cover tightly, and simmer for 20 minutes. Remove from the heat and allow the rice to rest, covered, for 7 to 10 minutes. Fluff the rice by gently running a fork through the kernels, and serve.

notes

When tomatoes are out of season, you can substitute 1 cup (165 g) canned tomatoes, or add a couple of tablespoons of tomato sauce to your rice if you'd like a more prominent red color.

To make this dish vegetarian, use vegetable stock.

mexican red rice
(opposite)

mexican white rice
(page 142)

I am proud to come from Mazatlán, Sinaloa, "*donde se rompen las olas (where the waves break)*," as the song "El Sinaloense" goes.

One of the things I love the most about our region of Mexico is that it is a port town and, thus, seafood is everywhere. This rice is the perfect accompaniment to some of my favorite seafood dishes. And it's also the one that I make for my vegetarian friends; I just use vegetable stock rather than chicken stock. Mexican white rice is an underrated preparation, but once you try it, you will become a fan. Trust me.

mexican white rice

ARROZ BLANCO MEXICANO

serves 4

1 tablespoon canola oil

1 cup (185 g) long-grain white rice

¼ small onion, minced

1 garlic clove, minced

Kernels from 1 ear of yellow corn (or ¾ cup/110 g drained canned or frozen corn)

1⅔ cups (405 ml) chicken stock or vegetable stock

1 teaspoon salt

» Heat the oil in a medium saucepan over medium heat. Add the rice and cook, stirring, until it is lightly golden all over. Add the onion and garlic and cook, stirring, for 1 minute, or until the onion is translucent. Add the corn and sauté for an additional 1 to 2 minutes.

» Pour in the stock, add the salt, and bring to simmer. Reduce the heat to low, cover tightly, and simmer for 20 minutes.

» Remove from the heat and allow the rice to rest for 7 to 10 minutes. Fluff the rice by gently running a fork through the kernels, and serve.

Along with Traditional Guacamole (page 129), traditional refried beans are one of the recipes I get the most requests for. Depending on where you come from in Mexico, "traditional refried beans" can mean many things, including soft saucy beans (*frijoles caldudos*) or dry refried beans, which are usually a day old, super-fatty, and ridiculously yummy. I started making my version of this side dish when I was just five years old and have been making it for more than twenty-seven years now. Back then, my mom was single, and I pitched in to learn how to make the basics for my little brother and me. My mom had lost her own mother at age seven, so she wanted to make sure I learned as much as I could at a young age. I am so grateful, because those early lessons shaped me into the chef that I am today. *Gracias, Mamita*.

traditional refried beans

FRIJOLES REFRITOS TRADICIONALES

makes about 3 cups (720 ml)

½ to ¾ cup (105 to 155 g) lard or vegetable shortening

3½ cups (600 g) cooked pinto or Peruvian beans (page 18), or use canned beans

1½ cups (360 ml) bean cooking liquid (or liquid from the can if using canned beans)

Salt, if needed

⊹ Place a deep skillet over medium-high heat. Add ½ cup (105 g) lard or shortening and heat until it is completely liquid and smoking. It is very important that it reaches the smoking point; this process is called *quemar la manteca* (burning the lard). Add the beans and bean liquid quickly to bring down the temperature of the oil and stop the oil from jumping. Bring the beans to a simmer.

⊹ Reduce the heat to low and simmer uncovered for 8 to 10 minutes. Continue to cook, mashing the beans constantly, for about 5 minutes, until you have a smooth consistency with no whole beans left and the mashed beans have thickened considerably. Add more bean cooking liquid if needed and season with salt if you wish. If you make your beans ahead of time, save some cooking liquid to thin them out a bit when you reheat them; they will thicken further as they sit.

(recipe continues)

⁂ For soft refried beans, remove them from the heat and serve. For dry refried beans, remove the beans from the heat, let them cool completely, and refrigerate overnight. The following day, add another ¼ cup (50 g) lard or shortening and bring it to the smoking point again. Place the beans in the skillet and bring them to a simmer over medium heat, then reduce the heat to low and fry the beans in the added fat for a second time until they are shiny and medium brown in color, 10 to 15 minutes. The beans will have lost some of their moisture from refrigerating; the fat gives added moisture and makes them darker and shinier.

notes

The dry refried beans version makes the best grilled taquitos. To make refried bean taquitos, spoon about 2 tablespoons of beans onto the middle of a tortilla as it's being warmed on a grill. Once the tortilla is soft and malleable, fold it in half, move it to the indirect heat area of the grill, and heat, flipping once or twice, until the tortilla is crisp on the outside. They are perfect served alongside Grilled Red Snapper (page 63).

If you are feeling adventurous and can come by pigs' ears (you can ask your butcher to special order them for you), I truly hope you will make this recipe—not only because the texture is unlike anything you have ever had before, but because the boiling liquid is infused with a depth of spices that can be tasted in each crunchy morsel. Just think of this dish as a kind of pork crackling and you will have no problem crunching away!

This snack is the perfect crunchy topping for pork cheek tostadas (see page 102) or as another crunchy facet to be added to any dish.

crispy pigs' ears

OREJA DE CERDO FRITA

serves 6 to 8

2 tablespoons annatto seeds

4 garlic cloves, peeled and crushed

2 tablespoons dried Mexican oregano

Salt

2 pigs' ears

Canola oil, for frying

⊁ Fill a large saucepan halfway with water and bring it to a boil over high heat. Reduce the heat to medium and add the annatto seeds, garlic, oregano, and 2 tablespoons salt.

⊁ Place the pigs' ears into the water and cover the pot. Reduce the heat to low and simmer for 2 hours, or until the cartilage can be pierced easily with a fork. Remove from the water to a plate and let the ears cool completely. (Don't place them on paper towels, as the gelatinous skin will stick and you will be unable to remove the paper.)

⊁ Cut the pigs' ears into ⅛- to ¼-inch (3- to 6-cm) -wide noodle-like strips.

⊁ Fill a deep pan with 1½ inches (4 cm) of oil and heat it to 350°F (175°C). Line a plate with paper towels or parchment paper and have it ready.

⊁ Carefully slip the pig ear strips into the oil, making sure they don't stick to each other. Fry for 2 to 3 minutes, until completely crisp. Remove them from the oil using a slotted spoon, place on the paper towel–lined plate, and immediately season with salt. Serve immediately.

My season of *MasterChef* featured some incredible ingredients, but there's one rarely seen in the *MasterChef* kitchen that I'm so glad I requested—pork skin!

Pork skin is a relatively uncommon ingredient, and that's why I knew I had to include pork chicharrón in my finale menu. This crispy treat is so humble and simple, yet so technically complex that it's difficult to complete it in sixty minutes. But where there is a will, there is a way— and this Latina sure found a way!

While there are a number of different types and textures of chicharrón in Mexican cuisine, I decided to make an ultra-crispy, sexy version to serve atop my Huitlacoche Tamales (page 82). There are many delicious ways to enjoy this treat. For starters, try it as an appetizer with salsa and fresh Mexican cheeses, serve it alongside an entrée to provide contrast in flavor and texture, crush it up and dust it over corn on the cob, or add it to salad for a little crunch.

crispy pork chicharrón

CHICHARRÓN CASERO

makes about 2 dozen

6 cups (1.4 L) hot water

¼ cup (60 g) coarse kosher salt, plus more for seasoning

1 pound (455 g) fresh pork skin

Canola oil, for frying

Tajin seasoning

⫸ Pour the hot water into a pressure cooker. Set it over medium-high heat until steaming. Add the salt and stir to dissolve it.

⫸ Cut the pork skin into 2 x 4-inch (5 x 10-cm) rectangles using a serrated or very sharp knife. Add it to the water, secure the pressure cooker with the lid according to the manufacturer's instructions, bring it to high pressure, and cook for 20 minutes. Remove from the heat and carefully release the pressure using the quick-release valve. If you do not have a pressure cooker, you can boil the pork skin in a stockpot for 45 to 60 minutes.

⫸ Remove the pork skin and lay it on a baking sheet to air-dry for 5 to 10 minutes (do not use paper towels, as they will stick to the pork skin).

✦ Meanwhile, fill a deep fryer or large pot with 3 inches (7.5 cm) of oil and heat it over medium-high heat to 385°F (195°C).

✦ Cut the skin diagonally from corner to corner, creating two even triangles.

✦ Working in batches, carefully place the pieces in the fryer, cover it immediately, and stand back, as the oil will start to sputter. Fry for 5 to 7 minutes, until the skins are crisp; you will know they are done when they are no longer popping and crackling and the oil is no longer splashing around. Your chicharrónes will be a gorgeous golden brown and just barely bubbling in the oil.

✦ Remove them to a parchment paper–lined baking sheet or plate and immediately season with salt and the Tajin (a mix of chiles, salt, and dehydrated lime juice; you want to get the seasoning on when the skin is still warm so that it sticks). Let them rest for a few minutes, then serve.

breakfast

DESAYUNO

There is no better way to start your morning than with spicy food to get your blood flowing, right? Reading through this chapter, you will quickly find out that many of us Mexicans feel this way. We add made-from-scratch salsa to just about everything to spice it up. In fact, I am pretty sure that your tolerance for spice will grow as you cook through this chapter and feast on some of the most intriguing rustic breakfasts found throughout many regions of Mexico. Rise and shine, everyone—things are just heating up!

We Mexicans sure come up with some funny names for foods, don't we? *Divorciados* simply describes eggs smothered in two different salsas. It's like two dishes in one, and it makes great use of leftover salsa you may have in your fridge. *Divorciados* are served with refried beans, along with a sprinkle of Cotija cheese, and warm tortillas on the side for dipping and scooping up all that delicious salsa.

divorced eggs

HUEVOS DIVORCIADOS

serves 4

½ cup (120 ml) Rustic Mexican Salsa (page 30)

½ cup (120 ml) Tomatillo Salsa (page 35)

Canola oil

8 large eggs

Salt and freshly ground black pepper

Traditional Refried Beans (page 143), warmed

Crumbled Cotija cheese

¼ cup (10 g) chopped fresh cilantro leaves

Corn or flour tortillas, homemade (see page 20 or 22) or store-bought

≫ Pour the two salsas into separate small saucepans and bring each to a simmer over low heat.

≫ Heat 1 tablespoon of the oil in a small nonstick skillet over medium-high heat. Crack 2 eggs into the skillet and cook them for 1 to 2 minutes, until the whites are set. Flip the eggs and fry them on the second side for 30 seconds. Remove them from the pan and set the eggs on opposite sides of a plate. Season with salt and pepper. Repeat with the remaining eggs, adding more oil to the pan as needed, until you have four plates with two eggs each.

≫ Place a line of warmed beans in the center of each plate between the eggs to create two sides to the plate. Smother the eggs with the warm salsas, using the rustic salsa on one side and the tomatillo salsa on the other side.

≫ Sprinkle some Cotija cheese over the beans. Garnish with cilantro and serve with tortillas alongside.

The first time I had *huevos en revoltillo,* we were visiting my step-grandparents in Tecate. I was seven years old, and it was the first night I had ever spent away from home. The next morning, I woke to the smell of onion wafting from the kitchen, and it was enough to pull me right out of bed. We had salsa-scrambled eggs for breakfast, and I was hooked. That recipe has stayed with me since that morning, and now I'm passing it on to you!

salsa-scrambled eggs

HUEVOS EN REVOLTILLO

serves 4

8 large eggs

1 tablespoon canola oil

½ small yellow onion, minced

1 cup (240 ml) Rustic Mexican Salsa (page 30), Tomatillo Salsa (page 35), or prepared salsa

Salt and freshly ground black pepper, to taste

» Crack the eggs into a large bowl (but do not whisk them).

» Heat the oil in a large nonstick skillet over medium-high heat. Add the onion and cook until it is almost crisp on the edges, 1 to 2 minutes. Add the salsa, bring it to a simmer, and reduce the heat to medium-low.

» Add the eggs to the pan and, using a wooden spoon, start mixing them in to break up the yolks quickly. The idea is to not completely whisk the eggs but to keep breaking them up and incorporating the salsa. Continue mixing for about 5 minutes, until the eggs are completely incorporated into the salsa and set to your liking. Season with salt and pepper if needed. Serve immediately.

Breakfast is by far my favorite meal of the day. I wanted to share a recipe that takes me back to when my stepdad, Martin, came into our lives. Before he came to us, it was just my brother, my mom, and me. We didn't know it at the time, but we were meeting the man who I would come to know as the only father I have in this world.

That day, he was sitting in our little kitchen nook enjoying the *huevos rancheros* my mom had just made, and I remember telling my brother, "He's crazy! Do you see all that salsa?" My dadito, as I call him, is a man's man, a true Mexican macho, and as such, loves a hearty breakfast. Therefore, know that this dish isn't for the weak . . . don't worry, you can do this.

salsa-smothered eggs

HUEVOS RANCHEROS

serves 4

About 1½ cups (360 ml) Rustic Mexican Salsa (page 30)

1 cup (240 ml) canola oil

4 corn tortillas, homemade (see page 20) or store-bought

8 large eggs

Salt

Traditional Refried Beans (page 143), warmed

Cotija cheese, crumbled

¼ cup (10 g) chopped fresh cilantro leaves

⁑ Pour the salsa into a medium saucepan. Place it over low heat and bring it to a simmer. This will take some time if your salsa has been refrigerated. Don't worry; just keep an eye on it as you multitask through the rest of the steps.

⁑ Heat the oil in an 8-inch (20-cm) nonstick skillet over medium heat until almost smoking. Pierce a small hole in each tortilla with a fork to keep them from puffing. Slowly add one tortilla to the skillet, making sure the oil fully covers the tortilla. Fry it on each side for about 1 minute, until semi-crisp and golden brown, pressing it down with tongs as needed to keep it submerged in the oil. Remove from the oil using tongs, allowing excess oil to drip off, and place it on a large paper towel–lined plate. Repeat until all the tortillas are fried.

⁑ Pour all but 1 tablespoon of the frying oil into a bowl, increase the heat to medium-high, and heat until it is almost smoking. Crack two eggs into the skillet and cook them for 1 to 2 minutes, until the whites are set. Flip the eggs and fry them on the other side for 1 additional minute. Remove them from the oil and place them on a plate. Continue adding oil and cooking two eggs at a time until you've cooked them all. Season each batch of fried eggs with salt as they're done.

⁑ To serve, place a tortilla on a plate and add two fried eggs. Smother them with some simmering salsa, add a side of refried beans and a little Cotija cheese, and garnish with cilantro. Serve immediately.

Green chilaquiles are like green enchiladas for breakfast! They are spicy, crunchy, and just so comforting. They remind me of weekend breakfasts at home with my mom. At my house, weekends were for real, hearty breakfasts with eggs and beans—the kind that would hold us over almost until dinnertime. Chilaquiles were my favorite breakfast, and the green variety, using tomatillo salsa, was my favorite type. The tartness of the tomatillo-based salsa works perfectly with the cool texture of Mexican *crema*. When I was lucky enough to get a fried egg on top, that was the best treat. A medium fried egg will have you screaming, "*Ay, yai, yai, yai*" like a mariachi singer!

green chilaquiles

CHILAQUILES VERDES

serves 4

1 cup (240 ml) canola oil

12 (6-inch/15-cm) corn tortillas, homemade (see page 20) or store-bought, cut into 1-inch (2.5-cm) squares using kitchen scissors (save the rounded ends too)

½ medium yellow onion, thinly sliced

4 garlic cloves, thinly sliced

1½ to 2 cups (360 to 480 ml) Tomatillo Salsa (page 35)

Cotija cheese, crumbled

Mexican crema or sour cream

✣ Heat the oil in a large, deep skillet over medium heat. Toss in a little piece of tortilla to test it: If it sizzles, it's ready. Add one-third of the tortilla squares and ends to the oil and fry until they're golden brown. Remove them with a slotted spoon to a paper towel–lined plate to absorb excess oil. Repeat with the remaining tortilla squares and ends, making sure to let the oil come back up to temperature between batches.

✣ Pour out all but 1 tablespoon of the frying oil from the pan, add the onion and garlic, and sauté until they are fragrant and translucent, about 5 minutes. Add the salsa and bring it to a simmer. Remove the skillet from the heat and fold in the tortilla chips until fully coated. Cover tightly and allow the pan to rest for 2 to 3 minutes for the chips to soak in the salsa. Uncover, fold them one final time, and serve the chilaquiles garnished with Cotija cheese and *crema*.

notes

You can use pretty much any homemade salsa for your chilaquiles, but if you're pressed for time, you can substitute a bottled salsa.

Try making "divorced" chilaquiles by using two different types of salsas. Serve them side by side on the plate, and voila!

If you ask Munchkin what she wants for breakfast at Grandma's house, nine times out of ten she will tell you *chorizo con huevos* (chorizo and eggs). One of my favorite ways to eat chorizo and eggs is in crispy corn tortilla tacos. This is one of those recipes that can be easily adapted based on what you have in your fridge or what cheese you prefer, but these tacos will have you wanting breakfast for lunch, or dinner, or even as a late-night snack!

chorizo and egg tacos

TAQUITOS DE CHORIZO CON HUEVOS

makes 12 tacos

1 teaspoon canola oil

4 ounces (115 g) fresh ground or packaged soft chorizo

4 large eggs

12 (6-inch/15-cm) corn tortillas, homemade (see page 20) or store-bought

8 ounces (225 g) Monterey Jack cheese, coarsely shredded

Rustic Mexican Salsa (page 30), Tomatillo Salsa (page 35), or a good bottled salsa

⊁ Heat the oil in a large nonstick skillet over medium heat. Add the chorizo, breaking it up with a wooden spoon, and stir until it is cooked through and darkened by about two shades, about 5 minutes. Reduce the heat to medium-low.

⊁ In a large bowl, beat the eggs. Add them to the chorizo and cook, stirring continuously, until they are nearly set, 4 to 5 minutes. Remove the pan from the heat and set aside.

⊁ Heat a large skillet or *comal* (tortilla griddle) over medium-high heat. Place a couple of tortillas on the skillet and cook for 1 minute, then flip them and cook for an additional minute, or until soft and pliable. Wrap them in a kitchen towel as they are heated to keep them warm. When all the tortillas have been heated, reduce the heat under the skillet to low.

⊁ Build your tacos by cupping your hand around a warm tortilla. Add some cheese and about 2 tablespoons of the chorizo and egg mixture. Fold the taco in half, place it on the skillet, and use the back of a spatula to press it down for about 15 seconds, until the taco stays shut on its own. Cook for about 2 minutes, then flip and cook for an additional 2 to 3 minutes, until the taco shell is hardened and crisp.

⚡ Carefully remove the taco from the skillet with the spatula and repeat with the remaining tortillas and filling, making two or three tacos at a time as you get more skilled at stovetop multitasking. *Cuidado* (careful)—the melted cheese inside will be hot! Serve the tacos with salsa; add some refried beans (see page 143) for a more substantial meal.

notes

If you live near a good butcher, you may be lucky enough to find freshly made chorizo. Just remember that fresh chorizo can vary in spiciness or chunkiness. Play with the recipe and use a little less chorizo if you want to cut down the spice level.

This is an easy recipe to turn to when you're making breakfast for lots of people, as you can cook the chorizo in advance; when you toast the tortillas on the skillet, it will reheat the chorizo.

I dream of opening my own restaurant someday, and part of what drives me is the idea of rectifying the misconception about what authentic Mexican food really is. There are delicious taco shops and amazing street food stalls popping up everywhere, and I love them as much as anyone. But many of their adaptations of classic dishes have lost their origins over time. Machaca is one of those dishes.

Simply put, *authentic* machaca is a shredded beef main dish that traditionally is never scrambled with eggs! In fact, machaca is usually served as a protein for dinner. Here, I'm sharing a traditional machaca recipe, the way I learned to make it. That said, feel free to serve it any time of day or night, and if you really want to, I won't mind if you go ahead and eat it with *fried* eggs, the way we truly eat machaca and eggs!

traditional machaca

MACHACA TRADICIONAL

serves 6

2 pounds (910 g) boneless beef chuck roast, cut into 2-inch (5-cm) cubes

6 black peppercorns

1 yellow onion, cut in half

1 tablespoon canola oil

2 garlic cloves, sliced

2 Anaheim chiles, sliced into ¼-inch (6-mm) rounds

1 large Roma tomato, chopped

Salt and freshly ground black pepper

≫ Bring a large saucepan of water to a boil. Add the chuck roast, peppercorns, and an onion half. Return to a simmer, then reduce the heat to medium-low and simmer until the beef is fork-tender, 60 to 90 minutes. Remove the beef to a cutting board and reserve ½ cup (120 ml) of the broth for later.

≫ Using two forks, shred the meat into a thin yarn-like texture (it is much easier to do this when the meat is still warm).

≫ Finely chop the remaining onion half. Heat the oil in a large skillet over medium-high heat. Add the chopped onion and the garlic and cook for 1 minute. Add the chiles and sauté for an additional minute, until they start to soften. Add the tomato and cook for 1 to 2 minutes, until softened. Add the shredded meat and mix to incorporate. Add the reserved broth, season with salt and pepper, and reduce the heat to low. Cover and simmer for an additional 5 minutes, adding more broth if needed to further moisten the meat. Turn off the heat and allow the meat to rest for 3 to 5 minutes before serving.

desserts

POSTRES

One of the things I love most about Mexican desserts is the sheer depth of flavor you can get with such simple ingredients. I am truly proud of this chapter, because I can honestly say that it was where I worked the hardest to get better. Like most home cooks, I am no pastry master. Therefore, when I got word I would be going to Los Angeles to fight for an apron, I knew I had to work on my desserts.

Season Five of *MasterChef* left its mark on me, and I recalled how well Courtney placed that year because she excelled at both cooking and baking. So I got to work and channeled my inner Courtney to come up with some amazing recipes. The techniques might not always be totally Mexican, but the desserts are definitely packed with Mexican flavor!

fresh watermelon drink (opposite)

cinnamon-rice drink (page 164)

hibiscus and cinnamon iced tea (page 165)

aguas frescas

I could think of no better way to start the dessert chapter than with three of my favorite *aguas frescas* (literally "cool waters" or "fresh waters"). These delicious drinks are a perfect way to enjoy a little something sweet as a dessert alternative. I hope you will try all three of these drinks, as they each have their own texture, character, and flavor profile.

If you love creamy, you will love the *horchata* rice milk drink. It's sweet, with a touch of cinnamon that your palate can't help but rejoice over. The watermelon *agua fresca* is my mom's favorite—refreshing and perfect for a hot summer day. And if you like spicy, you will love the hibiscus and cinnamon iced tea, made from the poaching liquid from my Hibiscus-Poached Pears (page 186). In my household, we waste nothing.

fresh watermelon drink

AGUA DE SANDIA

makes 2 quarts (2 L)

4 cups (600 g) cubed seedless watermelon

Sugar

Lime wedges

⚹ Place the watermelon in a blender and puree it. Pour the puree into a 2-quart (2-L) pitcher and add cold water almost to the top. Sweeten the drink with sugar to taste and serve it with lime wedges to squeeze into each serving.

cinnamon-rice drink

AGUA DE HORCHATA

makes 2½ quarts (2.5 ℒ)

1 stick Mexican cinnamon

2 cups (370 g) uncooked long-grain white rice

1 cup (200 g) sugar

1 (12-ounce/340-g) can evaporated milk

❧ In a small saucepan, combine 2 cups (480 ml) of water with the cinnamon. Bring to a boil and boil for 10 minutes. Remove from the heat and let the liquid cool completely.

❧ In a medium nonreactive bowl, combine the rice with the cinnamon tea and the boiled cinnamon stick. Add enough water to cover the rice by about 1 inch (2.5 cm). Cover with plastic wrap and allow it to rest at room temperature for 12 hours.

❧ Place the mixture in a blender, along with the cinnamon stick, and blend on medium-high speed for about 2 minutes, until completely smooth. Push the rice mixture through a fine-mesh strainer to extract as much rice milk as possible. You should only have a few bits of rice left (if you have too much whole rice, you should blend it further).

❧ Add the sugar and stir until dissolved, then add 6 cups (1.5 L) water and the evaporated milk to dilute. Serve over ice.

hibiscus and cinnamon iced tea

AGUA DE JAMAICA Y CANELA

makes about 2 quarts (2 L)

Hibiscus poaching liquid from Hibiscus-Poached Pears (page 186)

Sugar, if needed

✣ Cool the hibiscus poaching liquid to room temperature with the hibiscus still in it so it can impart all of its delicious flavor. Strain the liquid through a fine-mesh sieve into a pitcher and add about 1 quart (960 ml) of cold water to dilute it. Check the flavor as you add the water to make sure you don't dilute it too far. Add sugar if needed, but since this poaching liquid is already very sweet, you likely won't need any. Enjoy this refreshing iced tea with or without a shot of tequila!

When I made these corn tamales on the show, not many people under-stood why I would make a sweet tamale. Being able to give people more of an understanding about Mexican food made me so proud.

One thing to consider with this recipe is that corn is usually sweetest when it is in season, so try to prepare this recipe during corn season. This recipe will not work with canned or frozen corn; so much of the texture of these tamales is owed to the starch the fresh corn provides, and you'll need the fresh green corn husks to wrap the tamales.

sweet corn tamales

TAMALES DULCES DE ELOTE

makes 18 to 20 tamales

5 to 8 large ears yellow corn (to equal 4 cups/580 g corn kernels)

1 cup (130 g) instant corn masa flour, such as Maseca, plus more if needed

1 cup (200 g) sugar

1 tablespoon baking powder

1 tablespoon Mexican vanilla extract

Pinch of salt

¾ cup (180 ml) melted lard or vegetable shortening, cooled slightly

¼ cup (35 g) raisins

Mexican Chocolate Sauce (page 169; optional)

» To remove the husks from the corn, use a chef's knife to cut through the bottom of the ears just above where the cob meets the stalk. Gently remove the husks (they tear easily). Remove the corn silk, rinse the husks, and set them aside. Pull apart torn or smaller husks (starting at the widest part of the husk and pulling down) into ¼-inch (6-mm) strips; you'll use these later to seal the tamales.

» Cut the kernels from the cobs, place them in a food processor, and process until they are nearly smooth. Pour the puree into a large bowl. Depending on how ripe your corn is, your puree will be more or less juicy and the amount of masa flour you use will vary from batch to batch. Start by sprinkling in about ¾ cup (90 g) of the masa flour and mix it in with a spoon or your hands. Keep adding masa flour until the mixture is no longer watery and doesn't stick to your spoon. Mix in the sugar, baking power, vanilla, and salt, followed by the melted lard or shortening, taking care to let it cool enough before adding so it doesn't burn your hands. Fold in the raisins.

» Fill a pot fitted with a steamer basket with about 2 inches (5 cm) of water.

» Place a cornhusk in the palm of your hand with the narrowest part facing you and the waxy side of the husk facing up. Using a large spoon, scoop about ¼ cup (60 ml) of the dough into the center of the cornhusk (there's no need to spread it as you would for most tamales),

(recipe continues)

sweet corn tamales
(opposite)

mexican chocolate
sauce (page 169)

leaving a little room for expansion. Seal the tamale by bringing the long sides of the husk together and tucking one side in under the other, making sure there is no gap. Then fold the short end upward and the wide end downward to close the tamale. Using the cornhusk strips, tie the open ends of each side (the length of the tamale) closed, getting as close to the masa as possible. Last, tie a cornhusk strip around the middle, just tight enough to give the tamale what we call a *cintura* (waist).

✯ As you make each tamale, set it in the steamer basket on its folded bottom. When all the tamales are in the steamer, place a layer or two of the remaining cornhusks on top to cover the tamales completely. Cover the pot, set it over medium-low heat, and bring to a simmer. Steam the tamales for about 1 hour, checking every 20 minutes to see if the pot needs more hot water. Remove a tamale, let it rest for 1 minute, and check it; it's done when the cornhusk peels away from the filling with ease. If not, give them a few more minutes and you'll be in corn heaven! Serve them warm, with Mexican Chocolate Sauce, if desired.

Walking into the *MasterChef* pantry meant coming face-to-face with the best ingredients from all over the world. One ingredient I kept seeing was chocolate of all types—but not Mexican chocolate. I knew that if I was going to create a dessert for the judges that included Mexican chocolate, I was going to have to develop it from scratch.

This is the recipe for the Mexican chocolate sauce I made to go alongside my Sweet Corn Tamales (page 166). The judges loved it, and I was absolutely thrilled. This sauce can go with almost any dessert, so don't be afraid to use it. Try it instead of chocolate syrup on an ice cream sundae—you will love it!

mexican chocolate sauce

JARABE DE CHOCOLATE MEXICANO

makes about 2 cups (.5 ℒ)

8 ounces (225 g) bittersweet chocolate, chopped

2 tablespoons sugar

1 teaspoon ground Mexican cinnamon

¼ teaspoon freshly grated nutmeg

Pinch of cayenne pepper

Pinch of salt

1½ cups (360 ml) heavy cream

» Place the chocolate in a heat-resistant bowl and sprinkle the sugar, cinnamon, nutmeg, cayenne, and salt over it.

» In a small saucepan, bring the cream just to a simmer over low heat. Watch carefully and, once your cream just begins to bubble, pour it over the chocolate. Leave it undisturbed for 3 to 4 minutes, then mix with a rubber spatula until all the chocolate is melted. Let it sit for a few minutes to thicken and then serve. Store in an airtight container in the refrigerator for up to 1 week. To reheat, place over a double boiler and mix until smooth.

notes

If you don't have access to Mexican cinnamon, increase the amount of another type of cinnamon up to double to achieve that signature Mexican chocolate taste.

If whole nutmeg isn't available, you can substitute ground nutmeg, using up to twice the amount. Freshly ground nutmeg is more potent and a little bit goes a long way, so tread lightly to make sure the nutmeg doesn't overpower the cinnamon.

Conchas are a signature type of Mexican sweet bread, known for their seashell-like scores on a sweet crumb coating. If you have never had Mexican sweet bread, you are in for a treat. *Conchas* have the texture of a soft dinner roll, but with an irresistible sugar topping that will make you want to double the batch the next time around! This recipe gives you the option to make both standard white and chocolate *conchas*. Try both, and then decide on your favorite.

traditional mexican sweet bread

CONCHAS TRADICIONALES

makes twelve 4-inch (10-cm) conchas

FOR THE CONCHAS:

3½ cups (440 g) all-purpose flour, plus more if needed

½ teaspoon salt

2 tablespoons active dry yeast

⅔ cup (135 g) granulated sugar, divided

4 large eggs

1 cup (2 sticks/225 g) unsalted butter, at room temperature

Vegetable oil, as needed

TO MAKE THE CONCHAS:

↠ Clean a work surface large enough for kneading. Combine the flour and salt in a bowl and pour it onto your work area in a mound. Create a well in the center.

↠ Heat ½ cup (120 ml) water in a small saucepan over low heat until warm but not boiling. Pour the water into a nonmetallic bowl, add the yeast and 1 tablespoon of the granulated sugar, and stir to combine. The sugar will help to activate the yeast. Set it aside until the yeast mixture doubles in volume, about 5 minutes.

↠ Pour the yeast mixture into the well in the center of the flour. Add the eggs and mix using your hands until they are incorporated into the flour. Add the butter 1 tablespoon at a time, incorporating each addition into the dough before adding the next. Add the remaining sugar and continue to knead the dough until incorporated. Your dough will be soft and sticky. If it's too sticky, give it a little more flour to help it take shape, but do not add more than ½ cup (65 g) of additional flour.

↠ Knead the dough for 15 to 30 minutes to develop the gluten and form a very soft but cohesive ball (see Notes, page 172). Place the dough in a greased glass or nonmetallic bowl. Add a bit of oil to the dough, if necessary, and cover it with plastic wrap to make sure it does not develop a skin. Place it near your oven or in a warm spot so the heat will help the yeast to rise. Allow the dough to rise for 2 hours.

MEANWHILE, MAKE THE TOPPING:

✣ Sift the flour and confectioners' sugar into a large bowl. Add the butter and knead just until it is fully incorporated, so the heat of your hands won't continue to melt the butter. Divide the dough into two equal portions. Take one half of the dough and add the cocoa powder. Mix until the cocoa is well blended and the color is uniform. Wrap each portion of dough in plastic wrap and refrigerate them until ready to use.

TO FORM THE CONCHAS:

✣ After the dough has risen for 2 hours, remove it from the bowl. On a lightly floured work surface, roll the dough into a large baguette shape. Cut the dough into three equal pieces, then cut each of those into four equal pieces to make twelve equal pieces of dough.

✣ On a lightly floured surface, roll each piece into a ball. Drizzle a bit of oil on your hands, if needed, and continue to roll the ball between your hands until it is smooth and uniform. Using only your fingers, flatten the ball of dough into a patty shape that is about 1 inch (2.5 cm) thick. Place the dough patty on a parchment paper–lined baking sheet. Repeat with the remaining dough balls, allowing at least 2 inches (5 cm) between each patty. Cover with plastic wrap and set them in a warm, draft-free location to rise for an additional 30 minutes.

✣ Pull your topping from the refrigerator and allow it to come to room temperature while you wait, about 10 minutes. *Do not* set it by the oven.

✣ As the dough is rising, preheat the oven to 375°F (190°C).

TO ASSEMBLE THE CONCHAS:

✣ Line two baking sheets with plastic wrap. Cut both the chocolate and traditional white toppings into six equal pieces to make twelve pieces. Shape the pieces into balls and lay six balls onto each prepared baking sheet, leaving an equal amount of space between them. Cover with another layer of plastic wrap (so you're placing the balls of

(recipe continues)

FOR THE TOPPING:

½ cup (65 g) all-purpose flour

½ cup (65 g) unsifted confectioners' sugar

½ cup (1 stick/115 g) unsalted butter, softened, cut into walnut-size pieces

2 tablespoons unsweetened cocoa powder

topping between two sheets of plastic wrap). Using a tortilla press or the flat bottom of a plate, press the balls flat until they are big enough to cover the top of a dough patty. Carefully peel back the plastic wrap from each side of the topping. If the topping gets too soft, refrigerate it for 5 minutes and proceed again. Place the topping directly onto the dough patty and repeat until all twelve breads have been covered.

✣ Using a thin fillet or paring knife, score the surface of the topping. Begin at one edge and score outward, as if you were drawing claws, to create a shell-like design.

✣ Bake for 20 minutes, or until the bottoms are golden brown. Remove from the oven and allow the *conchas* to rest for about 3 minutes before serving. Store in an airtight container for up to 3 days.

notes

This recipe can also be made in a stand mixer fitted with the hook attachment. Follow the general instructions for the manual method, but let the mixer do the elbow work for you! Start mixing on low speed until the dry and wet ingredients are combined, then increase the mixer speed to high as you slowly add the butter. Continue to mix on high speed for 15 to 20 minutes, until the gluten in the dough is developed.

It's no secret that I come from humble beginnings. For eight years, my mom was on her own raising my brother and me, and during that time she often struggled to make ends meet. When I look back on that time, what is so remarkable is that we never worried about where our next meal was coming from. My mother made sure that food was always something to enjoy and never something to worry over, even if our grand feast for the evening was little more than rice and beans.

When a "Mystery Box Challenge" on *MasterChef* featured rice, my mind immediately went to my childhood. I thought of those nights when adding chicken or steak to our dinner was simply not an option, when my mother walked through the door exhausted from a long day at work to find two eager mouths awaiting her, and she would make us rice pudding for dinner. These were the times when love conquered hunger and a warm bowl of rice meant mom was home, our bellies were full, and everything was going to be all right.

This is a sweet Mexican take on the classic Italian *arancini* (stuffed and fried rice balls). It is clearly very different, but when I was thinking of ways to elevate *arroz con leche*, the Italian rice ball came to mind, and voilà, *molotes de arroz con leche*!

rice pudding balls

MOLOTES DE ARROZ CON LECHE

makes about 18

2 cups (370 g) long-grain white rice, divided

2½ cups (600 ml) hot water

1 (12-ounce/340-g) can evaporated milk

1 stick Mexican cinnamon

¾ cup (150 g) sugar

Pinch of salt

½ cup (75 g) raisins

Canola oil, for frying

≫ In a spice grinder, grind 1 cup (185 g) of the rice to the texture of table salt, with some slightly coarser grains for texture. Transfer it to a shallow dish (see Notes, page 175).

≫ Place the hot water and evaporated milk in a medium saucepan. Add the cinnamon, place the saucepan over medium heat, and bring to a simmer. Add the remaining 1 cup (185 g) whole rice and the sugar and salt and bring it back to a simmer, stirring until the sugar has dissolved. Reduce the heat to low, cover, and cook for 20 minutes, removing the lid and stirring every 4 to 6 minutes to keep the rice from sticking to the bottom of the pot.

≫ Carefully fold in the raisins and cook the pudding uncovered for about another 15 minutes, stirring often, until the liquid is totally

(recipe continues)

absorbed into the rice and the rice is cooked through and soft but not mushy. Remove and discard the cinnamon stick and let the rice cool uncovered for 5 minutes.

❯ Line half of a baking sheet with plastic wrap. Scoop the rice from the pan onto the lined sheet in an even layer. Let it cool for a few minutes, then place it in the freezer for 5 to 8 minutes, until it is completely cooled but not frozen (if freezer space doesn't allow or you've got time to spare, you can cool the rice pudding completely on the countertop or in the refrigerator).

❯ Using a large kitchen spoon, scoop out a heaping spoonful of rice and, with your hands, form it into an oval shape roughly 1½ inches (4 cm) in diameter and 2 inches (5 cm) long (this shape is called a *molote*). Be careful not to overwork it, as the heat from your hands can melt the milk. Place the ball in the dish filled with ground rice and roll it around until covered generously. Repeat to make about eighteen rice pudding balls, placing them on a chilled, parchment paper–lined baking sheet as you form each one.

❯ Heat a deep fryer or high-sided skillet with at least 4 inches (10 cm) of oil to 375°F (190°C). Drop in a few rice balls, making sure there is plenty of space between them; do not overcrowd the pan. Fry for 3 to 5 minutes, until they are browned all over. Using a slotted spoon, remove them from the oil and place them on a baking sheet lined with a fresh sheet of parchment or paper towels. Repeat with the remaining rice balls, letting the oil come back up to temperature before adding each batch. Let them cool for a couple of minutes, then serve.

notes

If you don't have a spice grinder, you can simply toss the rice pudding balls in rice flour to coat before frying them; you won't get the rustic texture of grinding your own, but they'll still be delicious.

You can form the rice pudding into balls and freeze them for frying at a later time. Lay the balls out on a parchment paper–lined baking sheet, place it in the freezer, and freeze just until the balls are solid, about 1 hour, then pop them into a freezer bag for storage. Thaw them completely at room temperature before rolling them in the rice flour and frying.

Churros are one of the simplest of desserts to make, but for some reason most people will shy away from making them. I encourage you to give them a try, and don't fret if your churro-shaping skills aren't perfect. Trust me, there has never been a churro that was too ugly to eat! Any imperfections will be coated in the dust of the heavens, sugar and cinnamon. My churros are pinwheel shaped, instead of the traditional long wands, which the kids will get a kick out of.

churro pinwheels

PIRUELAS DE CHURRO

makes 12 pinwheels

Canola oil, for frying

1 cup (200 g) sugar

2 tablespoons ground cinnamon

1 cup (240 ml) whole milk

4 tablespoons (½ stick/55 g) unsalted butter

1 teaspoon salt

2 cups (250 g) all-purpose flour

》 Pour at least 1 inch (2.5 cm) of oil into a wide saucepan over medium heat and bring it to 375°F (190°C).

》 Combine the sugar and cinnamon in a large shallow bowl or rimmed plate and mix until incorporated.

》 In a medium saucepan, combine the milk, 1 cup (240 ml) water, the butter, and the salt. Place them over medium heat and warm until the butter has melted and the liquid just comes to a simmer. Remove the pan from the heat.

》 In one quick addition, add the flour. Using a wooden spoon, stir until it is well incorporated and smooth. The texture of the dough will be firm but malleable. Allow the dough to cool for 2 to 3 minutes in the pan.

》 Fit a pastry bag with a large closed star tip, fill the bag with warm churro dough, and begin piping it into the hot oil. Hold the bag a few inches above the oil, being careful to not burn yourself. To make a spiral, begin by creating a "D" shape, then proceed in a continuous circular motion, stopping when you have gone around 2 or 3 times to create a 4- to 6-inch (10- to 15-cm) spiral. Using a paring knife or kitchen scissors, cut the churro dough away from the piping bag. Fry it for 1½ minutes, or until golden brown on top. Using tongs, flip the churro over and continue to cook until it is golden brown on the second side. Using the tongs, remove the churro and place it onto a parchment paper– or paper towel–lined baking sheet to drain excess oil.

⚡ Quickly move the churro to the cinnamon-sugar mixture, quickly flip it, and place it on a serving plate. Repeat with the remaining dough to make twelve churros. Let them cool slightly and then serve.

notes
The technique for making churros is similar to making doughnuts, but know that churros are meant to be crispy on the outside and soft, creamy, and light like a popover on the inside.

Certain smells have always been nostalgic to me. Coffee reminds me so much of my *abuelito* Rogelio. When my mom would take us to visit our *abuelos* (grandparents) in Tijuana, we would get up early and pile into the car.

I can still smell the wafting scent of coffee as we crossed the threshold of their front door. Abuelito Rogelio sat in his usual corner right by the china cabinet and next to the back door. Newspaper in hand, he would peek over and give us the warmest smile in the world. My *abuelita* might have been grumbling about something in the kitchen, but when we saw my grandfather, his whole face lit up, and there was his coffee, sitting right in front of him.

I dedicate this recipe to my *abuelo*, who loved his coffee and whom I sorely miss. I think of him every time I make it.

mexican coffee flan

FLAN CAFÉ DE OLLA

serves 8

FOR THE CARAMEL:

1 cup (200 g) sugar

FOR THE ESPRESSO CUSTARD:

¼ cup (30 g) Nescafe Café de Olla instant coffee powder

1 (12-ounce/340-g) can evaporated milk

6 large eggs

¾ cup (150 g) sugar

1 (14-ounce/400-g) can sweetened condensed milk

1 tablespoon Mexican vanilla extract

⸭ Preheat the oven to 350°F (175°C).

TO MAKE THE CARAMEL:

⸭ In a medium saucepan, bring ½ cup (120 ml) water to a simmer over medium-low heat. Add the sugar and swirl the pan to combine. Increase the heat to medium-high and cook until a medium-brown caramel forms, about 12 minutes, occasionally swirling the pan to color the caramel evenly. Remove it from the heat and divide the caramel among eight (6-ounce/180-ml) ramekins or silicone molds, swirling to make sure the bottoms and parts of the sides are fully coated.

⸭ Bring a kettle of water to a boil.

TO MAKE THE ESPRESSO CUSTARD:

⸭ In a small bowl, whisk the coffee powder into the evaporated milk. In a large bowl, whisk together the eggs and sugar until the sugar is fully dissolved. Add the coffee-flavored evaporated milk, sweetened condensed milk, and vanilla and whisk to incorporate. Strain through a fine-mesh strainer into a large pitcher (this removes air bubbles).

(recipe continues)

❧ Very slowly fill each ramekin about two-thirds full with the custard mixture. Place the ramekins in a shallow baking pan and place it in the oven. Carefully pour the boiling water into the pan to come halfway up the sides of the ramekins. Cover the pan with aluminum foil and bake for about 40 minutes, until the custards are just set and tremble in the center a little when shaken. Use tongs to carefully remove the custards from the water bath and place them on a wire rack to cool completely, about 30 minutes. Cover each one with plastic wrap and refrigerate them for at least 4 hours to chill (you can prepare the flans a day or two ahead).

❧ To unmold the flans, place the molds in a pan with 1 inch (2.5 cm) of warm water for 5 minutes. Loosen the custard by running a sharp, thin knife around the inside of the ramekins and place a rimmed plate upside down on top of each. Invert the plates, carefully lift the ramekins off to remove them and reveal the caramel, and serve.

"*Queremos pastel, pastel, pastel!* (We want cake, cake, cake!)"

I grew up hearing this chant, which was always followed by the typical Mexican birthday song "Las Mañanitas" and a pretty awesome homemade cake.

Although this cake was a family tradition when I was growing up, it was not my favorite treat. I felt that the bakers got a bit overzealous with the milk soak, to the point that the bread became a dripping, goopy, unappetizing mess.

I was absolutely thrilled when I had the opportunity to make this cake for the judges during the celebration of the 100th episode of *MasterChef*! This was my chance to make this traditional cake as I'd always imagined it—and, of course, to make it *MasterChef*-worthy! I set out to create a *pastel tres leches* recipe that was refined but still packed the punch of the amazing flavors I grew up with. When you eat it, I hope you'll do the chant and think of me!

tres leches birthday cake

PASTEL TRES LECHES

makes 1 (8-inch/20-cm) three-layer cake

FOR THE CAKE:

4½ cups (585 g) cake flour, plus more for the pans

3½ teaspoons baking powder

2 teaspoons kosher salt (see Notes)

1½ cups (3 sticks/340 g) unsalted butter, softened

(ingredients continue on page 184)

≫ Preheat the oven to 350°F (175°C).

MAKE THE CAKE:

≫ Butter and line three 8 x 2-inch (20 x 5-cm) round cake pans with parchment paper and dust them with cake flour, tapping out the excess. In a large bowl, sift together the flour, baking powder, and salt.

≫ In another large bowl using an electric mixer, beat the butter, granulated sugar, and brown sugar on medium-high speed. Using a rubber spatula, scrape the inside edges of the bowl and continue to beat with the mixer until the mixture is light and fluffy, 5 to 8 minutes. Reduce the mixer speed to low and mix in the eggs one at a time until well incorporated, about 3 minutes. Slowly pour in the oil and mix until well

(recipe continues on page 184)

tres leches birthday
cake (page 181)

2¾ cups (550 g) granulated sugar

¼ cup (55 g) packed light brown sugar

6 large eggs

⅔ cup (165 ml) grapeseed oil

1 cup (240 ml) whole milk

2 tablespoons vanilla extract

FOR THE FROSTING:

8 ounces (225 g) cream cheese, softened

1½ cups (3 sticks/340 g) unsalted butter, softened

2 pounds (910 g) confectioners' sugar, sifted

1 teaspoon vanilla extract

¼ cup (60 ml) fresh lemon juice

Zest of 1 lemon

FOR THE TRES LECHES SOAK:

1 cup (240 ml) sweetened condensed milk

¾ cup (180 ml) evaporated milk

¾ cup (180 ml) whole milk

FOR THE FILLING:

2 ripe bananas, sliced ¼ inch (6 mm) thick

1 pound (455 g) fresh strawberries, hulled and sliced ¼ inch (6 mm) thick (see Notes)

blended, about 1 minute. Add the dry ingredients, alternating with the milk (add the vanilla with the first milk addition), starting and ending with the dry ingredients, mixing only until the ingredients are incorporated before adding the next addition and scraping down the bowl between additions as needed. Turn the mixer to high speed and beat the batter for 4 minutes, or until it is fluffy and well aerated.

» Divide the batter among the three pans and level the batter smooth using a small, offset metal spatula. Remove any extra air bubbles by tapping the baking pans hard on a countertop three or four times. Bake until the cakes pull away from the sides of the pans and the centers are soft but firm to touch, about 35 minutes. Set the cakes on a wire rack and allow them to cool for 10 minutes. Run a small, offset metal spatula or knife around the inside edges of the pans and invert the cakes onto wire racks to cool completely; peel off the parchment. When cooled, cut the dome off of each cake so you have three even cake layers.

MAKE THE FROSTING:

» In a large bowl with a mixer, beat the cream cheese and butter at medium speed until smooth. Reduce the mixer speed to low and incorporate the confectioners' sugar in ½-cup (65-g) increments. Turn the mixer off and add the vanilla, lemon juice, and lemon zest. Beat for 1 minute, or until combined, then increase the mixer speed to medium-high and beat until the frosting is light and fluffy, 1 to 2 minutes.

MAKE THE TRES LECHES SOAK:

» In a medium bowl, whisk all three milks together and refrigerate until ready to use.

BUILD THE CAKE:

» Place the first layer of cake onto a cake stand cut-side up. Pierce it evenly across the top with the tines of a fork, making plenty of room for the milk soak to penetrate. Using a pastry brush, apply one-third of the milk soak, making sure the cake absorbs it all. The cake should be moist but not dripping with liquid.

» Spread one-third of the frosting on top of the first cake layer. Using half of the strawberry and banana slices, arrange a single layer of alternating slices, setting the fruit close together. Add the second cake layer, pierce it, and brush another third of the milk soak over it. Top with another third of the cream cheese frosting and the remaining strawberry and banana slices. Add the final cake layer cut-side down, pierce it, and brush it with the remaining milk soak. Add a very thin layer of frosting to the top and sides of the cake with some of the remaining frosting (this is called a crumb coat; it traps any loose crumbs from the top of the cake and allows the final frosting to go on smoothly and cleanly without picking up any crumbs). Refrigerate the cake, uncovered, for 30 to 45 minutes, then use the remaining frosting to frost and decorate the top and sides of the cake.

notes

This recipe calls for a higher amount of salt than most cake recipes; I did this to balance out the sweet milk soak and frosting.

If your strawberries are too tart or not flavorful enough, sprinkle them with 1 tablespoon granulated sugar and set them aside to macerate for up to 5 minutes before arranging them on the cake.

You can decorate your cake any way you like. When I was on the show, I added two drops of yellow food coloring to half of the decorating frosting to create a different color pattern on the cake and to write *Feliz 100* (Happy 100). Adding edible flowers is another way to make your tres leches cake a memorable one.

That's right, I signed the plate! Because I wanted to sign off on the show and sign an endorsement of my menu. Each dish really felt like me on a plate, and I wanted to let the judges know that this red-headed Latina wasn't holding back. I wanted to win this thing!

With that idea in mind, I wanted something on the plate that screamed "Claudia," and what does that more than something red? My goal was to create a dish that was vibrant and passionate and that brought a punch of flavor. That mind-set lead me to this recipe. When you taste this dish I hope you can feel the passion I poured into creating it. For the finale, I served it alongside a vibrant Key Lime Flan (page 190), topped with Pepita Brittle and Maldon Salt (page 192), and garnished with marigold flower petals.

hibiscus-poached pears

PERAS EN ALMIBAR DE JAMAICA

serves 4

2 tablespoons unsalted butter

4 Forelle or other small firm, ripe pears, peeled

¼ cup (60 ml) tequila, preferably silver

1 (7-ounce/200-g) cone *piloncillo* (mexican brown sugar)

1 cup (200 g) granulated sugar

2 cups (85 g) dried hibiscus flowers

1 stick Mexican cinnamon

6 whole cloves

Edible marigold flowers (optional)

⯈ Melt the butter in a large sauté pan over medium-high heat. Add the pears and brown them on both sides, about 5 minutes, taking care not to let the butter burn. Carefully add the tequila to the pan, ignite it with a long kitchen match, and flambé to burn off the alcohol. Stay close by the pan and continue to cook until the flames extinguish and the tequila has evaporated completely, about 5 minutes. Remove the pears from the pan and set aside.

⯈ Fill a medium saucepan with 6 cups (1.4 L) water, add the *piloncillo*, and bring it to a simmer over medium-high heat. Reduce the heat to medium and heat until the sugar has dissolved, using a wooden spoon to carefully help it along. Add the granulated sugar, hibiscus, cinnamon stick, and cloves. Return to a simmer, then reduce the heat to medium-low and simmer for 10 minutes.

⯈ Add the pears and reduce the heat to low to ensure that the liquid is just at a bare simmer. Poach the pears for 25 to 35 minutes (timing varies based on the size and ripeness of your pears), until the tines of a fork enter a pear effortlessly. Pull the pears out carefully using a ladle or slotted spoon, brush off any hibiscus clinging to the pears, and set them aside on a plate to rest.

✳ Strain out 1 cup (240 ml) of the poaching liquid (save the rest to make Hibiscus and Cinnamon Iced Tea, page 165). Pour the liquid into a small skillet or sauté pan, set it over medium heat, and reduce the liquid by about two-thirds. To check if your syrup is ready, dip the back of a spoon in the syrup and run another spoon through it; if it leaves a trail through the sauce, you are good to go. Immediately remove from the heat and let it cool slightly (it will thicken some more as it sits).

✳ To serve, slice the pears in half lengthwise and scoop out the seeds with a melon baller or spoon, revealing their bright yellow interior. If needed, cut a slice off of the bottom of each pear half to help them stand upright.

✳ Decorate the plates with the syrup using a spoon, or simply smother your poached pears in it. Garnish with marigold flowers, if available.

notes

For perfectly poached pears, try a trick I used during the finale: Cut out a circle of parchment paper to fit snugly into the pan, make a cut in the middle of the circle to allow steam to escape, and place it on top of the pears to keep them submerged.

Save your poaching liquid! One of my favorite drinks is an iced hibiscus tea we call *agua fresca de jamaica*. Using this poaching liquid as your base is a bit different from a typical *agua de jamaica* because it includes the spiciness of cinnamon and cloves, but I assure you, you will want to drink it all up. It's perfect for the holidays! See the recipe on page 165.

hibiscus-poached
pears (page 186)

key lime flan
(page 190)

pepita brittle
with maldon salt
(page 192)

As anyone who watched the show knows, things haven't always been easy for me. However, even through tough times, the support of my parents and the values they have instilled in me have shaped me into the strong fighter I am today. I may be tart at times, but I am bright and vibrant like the Key limes used in this delicious flan.

This dish was part of my finale dinner. I topped it with Pepita Brittle with Maldon Salt (page 192) to provide the contrast in texture and flavor that completed the dessert. I have often thought of this dish as a representation of my journey—the story of a woman who is unwilling to allow the trials of her life to turn her sour, and instead manages to remain sweet and vibrant.

key lime flan

FLAN DE LIMA

serves 6

FOR THE CARAMEL:

2 tablespoons fresh lime juice, preferably from Key limes

¾ cup (150 g) sugar

FOR THE CUSTARD:

1 (14-ounce/400-g) can sweetened condensed milk

1 (12-ounce/340-g) can evaporated milk

1½ teaspoons vanilla extract

3 large eggs

⤳ Preheat the oven to 275°F (135°C).

TO MAKE THE CARAMEL:

⤳ In a medium saucepan, bring 3 tablespoons of water and the lime juice to a simmer over medium-low heat. Add the sugar and swirl the pan to combine. Increase the heat to medium-high and cook until it is lightly golden in color, 5 to 7 minutes, occasionally swirling the pan to color the caramel evenly. Remove it from the heat and divide the caramel among six (6-ounce/180-ml) ramekins or silicone molds, swirling to make sure the bottoms and parts of the sides are fully coated.

⤳ Bring a kettle of water to a boil.

TO MAKE THE CUSTARD:

⤳ In a separate medium saucepan, combine the condensed milk and evaporated milk. Place the mixture over medium-high heat and bring to the scalding point; do not let it boil. Add the vanilla and immediately remove the pan from the heat.

⤳ In a medium bowl, beat the eggs. Temper the eggs by slowly pouring in the hot milk mixture a little at a time, while whisking vigorously. Strain the mixture into a clean bowl and add the lime juice and zest.

≫ Very slowly fill each ramekin about three-quarters full with the custard. Place the ramekins in a shallow baking pan and place it in the oven. Carefully pour the boiling water into the pan to come halfway up the sides of the ramekins. Cover the pan with aluminum foil and bake for about 40 minutes, until the custards are just set and tremble in the center a little when shaken. Use tongs to carefully remove the custards from the water bath and place them on a wire rack to cool completely, about 30 minutes. Cover each one with plastic wrap and refrigerate them for at least 4 hours to chill (you can prepare the flans a day or two ahead).

≫ To unmold the flans, place the molds in a pan filled with 1 inch (2.5 cm) of warm water for 5 minutes. Loosen the custard by running a sharp knife around the inside of the ramekins and place a rimmed plate upside down on top of each. Invert the plates and carefully lift the ramekins off to remove them and reveal the caramel. Serve them topped with pieces of pepita brittle.

notes

Custards need and deserve love. Cool them as long as you can before unmolding so that your custards keep their shape and don't break. During the *MasterChef* finale, I didn't have the luxury of time, so if you are in a hurry, you can unmold your custards as soon as 5 minutes after removing them from the oven. Just be very careful while coaxing them out of the ramekins.

2 tablespoons fresh lime juice, preferably from Key limes

1 tablespoon lime zest, preferably from Key limes

Pepita Brittle with Maldon Salt (page 192)

My relationship with my stepdad has had a large and amazing influence on me. He introduced me to so many new foods, and one of them was *pepitas* (pumpkin seeds). Pumpkin seeds are my dad's favorite salty snack, and when I was growing up, every autumn he would scoop out the seeds from our pumpkins and toast them with my brother and me.

It was this memory that I was channeling during the *MasterChef* finale when I created my recipe for pepita brittle. In Mexico, pepita brittle is made from a simple caramelized sugar, and serving this crunchy caramel with my Key Lime Flan (page 190) provided the added texture to my dessert to help make it a success.

pepita brittle with maldon salt

PEPITORIA CON SAL MALDON

makes about 9 ounces (255 g)

⅓ cup (45 g) unsalted hulled pepitas

1 teaspoon Maldon or other coarse sea salt

1 cup (200 g) sugar

3 tablespoons unsalted butter

⚹ Heat a medium skillet over medium heat. Add the pepitas and toast them for 2 to 3 minutes, tossing constantly, until they turn two to three shades darker. Take care not to let them burn.

⚹ Line a baking sheet with a silicone baking mat or parchment paper and have your toasted pepitas and salt ready to use in small bowls.

⚹ Combine the sugar and butter in a small saucepan (preferably nonstick) over medium-low heat. Cook, stirring, until the caramel reaches 290°F (145°C) and prepare to move quickly! Remove the pan from the heat and quickly pour the caramel directly onto the silicone baking mat, moving the pan around to coat the mat as thinly as possible, covering about three-quarters of the mat. Immediately sprinkle the pepitas across the top, but do not overcrowd them. Strategically scatter the salt in between the pepitas so it's evenly distributed. The effect you want is for the pepitas and salt to look as though they are floating on top of the brittle.

⁂ Let the brittle cool for a few minutes, then place the pan in the freezer for 5 minutes, or until it is completely cooled. Remove it from the freezer, pick up the silicone baking mat from the corner, separate the brittle from the mat, and crack it into desired shapes. (Breaking the candy this way gives you more control over the size and shape of the pieces.) Store in an airtight container for up to 2 weeks.

notes

You can grind up some pepita brittle in a spice grinder (or wrap it in cheesecloth and pound it with a meat tenderizer) to make a hard candy pepita dust. Use it to line the rim of a cocktail glass, sprinkle it on ice cream, or add it to your favorite custard dessert. Your guests will never expect the sweet and salty surprise.

acknowledgments

AGRADECIMIENTOS

Nothing could have prepared me for this moment in life, a moment when triumph is finally mine, when freedom is finally attainable, and when healing is finally possible. For this reason, I have to say, *Gracias mi Dios. Tal vez un día te pueda dar el abrazo mas grande del mundo por darme este dichoso éxito.*

I would like to thank my book team, Edwin, Thomas, Samantha, Leda, Danielle, and the whole Abrams team. Thank you for your patience with me and for making this book what I envisioned. You were right, it turned out perfect.

Thank you, Chef Gordon Ramsay, for never letting up on me and pushing me to excellence. You are an incredible mentor and I promise to have no more dreams of you again. Maybe.

Thank you, Chef Graham Elliot, for reminding me to focus on who I am and staying true to myself. You were right, that hard time was but a moment in time, and the sacrifice was WELL worth it.

Thank you, Chef Christina Tosi, for your advice, your confidence, and your energy. You are as genuine as you are fierce. It was an honor to learn from you.

Thank you, Adeline Ramage Rooney, for EVERYTHING. When are we going to Mazatlán?

Thank you to Stephanie Lewis, Yasmin Shackleton, and Robin Ashbrook for casting me for this amazing opportunity. This wouldn't be possible without you. Thank you for seeing my passion, drive, and potential.

To Chef Sandee Birdsong, Chef Avery Pursell, and the entire culinary team, *GRACIAS!* You all pushed me to be the best version of myself. Thank you for embracing my culinary dreams of an elevated Mexican cuisine and for finding the rarest of ingredients.

To the production and A.D. teams under Brian Smith (GOD), Anna, and Brady—you are all so incredibly talented and work so hard. Thanks for all you do.

A huge *gracias* to the teams at Endemol Shine, H&M Communications, Triple 7 PR, One Potato Two Potato, FOX, and Abrams.

A huge thank-you to my friends Steph, Mikey, and the rest of the wrangler crew: Thanks for the laughs and patience. Steph and Mikey, you two were my best friends and I am so thankful for the friendships we built.

A Humungadocious thank-you to Diane Cu, Todd Porter, and team. Thank you for the most incredible food photography I have ever seen, for embracing me and my family, and for understanding my vision and true identity.

Thanks to Amanda Saab: You kept me sane through this writing, you kept me going, thank you for helping me focus and for just being you.

To my MC Family: Nick, Ailsa, Tommy, Derrick, Stephen, Katrina, and the rest of the top 22, Top 40, and Top 100 . . . you are all rock stars! NEVER give up on your culinary dream.

Huge thanks to Lauren Gallaway: If it weren't for you, this journey would have never even been possible.

To Ilo Neukam and Jess Lawrence, thank you for pushing me beyond my excuses and reminding me that I deserved this opportunity.

To my i.d.e.a. family, thank you for the support and encouragement.

To Mike Fennessy, thank you for being my personal creative director and for helping me explain the vision in my head. You are such an incredible friend and I am so blessed to have you.

To Amy Lorenzen, Julie Messing-Paea, and Indra Gardiner-Bowers: You three women inspire me so much and I am blessed to have such successful women as mentors. *Gracias* for your support and encouragement.

Thank you to my prep team, Melanie Rose Prince and Anna Sciarrino. The amount of cooking practice I did with you two was invaluable. Thank you.

To Tania and Eily, thank you for always having my back and being not just friends but sisters. I am so glad you came into my life. Pretty sure I would have lost it without you two by now.

To my cousins Esmy, David, Rosy, and Juan, thank you for keeping me sane through this process.

To my brother and sisters, Josue, Marlia, and Liamar, I love you and hope I make you proud. Top that bishes!

Para mi Lita Hermelinda, gracias Abuelita por compartir su sazon y sus recetas conmigo. Espero este orgullosa de mi y este triunfo que lo comparto con usted y mi Abuela Coti. La adoro. Que dios me la bendiga.

Dadito, gracias papito lindo por ser una persona que me enseño lo que es ser papa de los buenos, amigo cuando te necesitaba, provee-dor cuando ya no podía, y mi constante recordatorio de ser paciente conmigo misma, con mis anhelos, y durante mis mas grandes frustra-ciones. Muchos de mis valores de trabajo vienen de ti. Mucho de mi éxito y triunfo han sido gracias a tus enseñanzas y valores. Gracias por ser mi Daddy, Mi Papi, y mi Dad. Te adoro.

Gracias Mami, for sharing all of your amazing recipes with me from a small age. This is OUR *triunfo*. A publishing of our family's recipes. *Un libro que afirma que todo lo que hemos pasado por nuestras vida fue con el propósito de llevarnos a este éxito. Mas que nada, espero que estés orgullosa de mi. Que este libro sea prueba que eres una de las mejores madres del mundo. Gracias por tu apoyo, por darme los valores con los que vivo mi vida con mi frente en alto. Por Nosotras!*

Lastly, thank you Yani, my sweet baby. This book took me away from you for so many days, hours, weeks, months. Never once did you ever judge me. I am not sure how I ever got this lucky. You are the most amazing child I could have ever had. You are the better part of anything I am. You are my best friend baby, my heart, my breath, my everything. This is just the beginning for us, honey. I can't wait to show you the world you deserve, Munchkin. Thank you for allowing me to be your mommy.

index

ÍNDICE

Page references in *italics*
refer to photographs